TATTOO
COLOURING BOOK

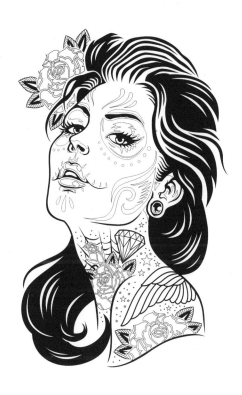

TATTOO
COLOURING BOOK

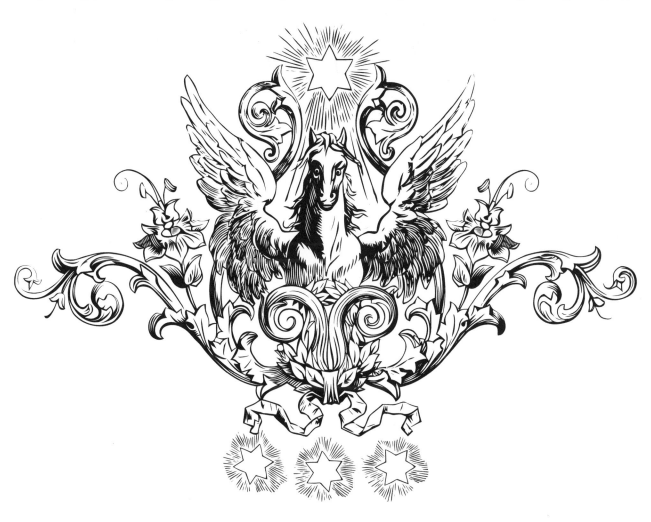

ARCTURUS

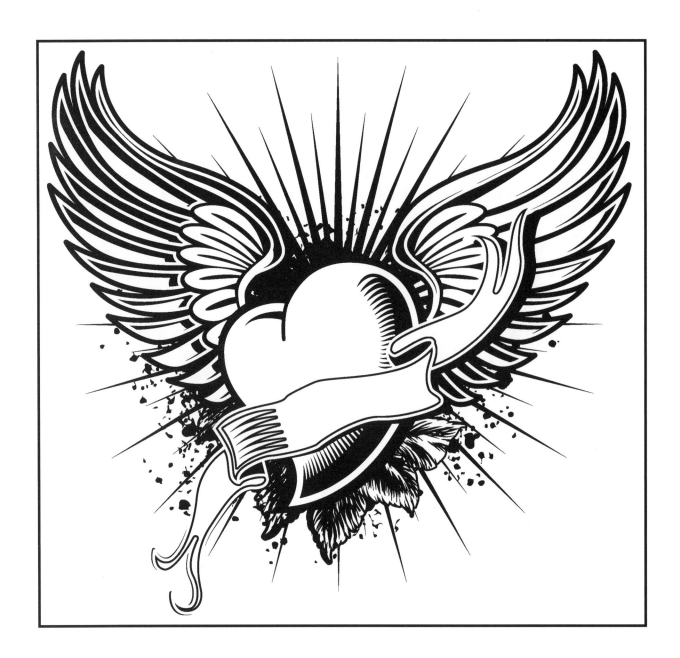

ARCTURUS

This edition published in 2015 by Arcturus Publishing Limited
26/27 Bickels Yard, 151–153 Bermondsey Street,
London SE1 3HA

Copyright © Arcturus Holdings Limited

ISBN: 978-1-78212-234-0
AD003574NT

Printed in China

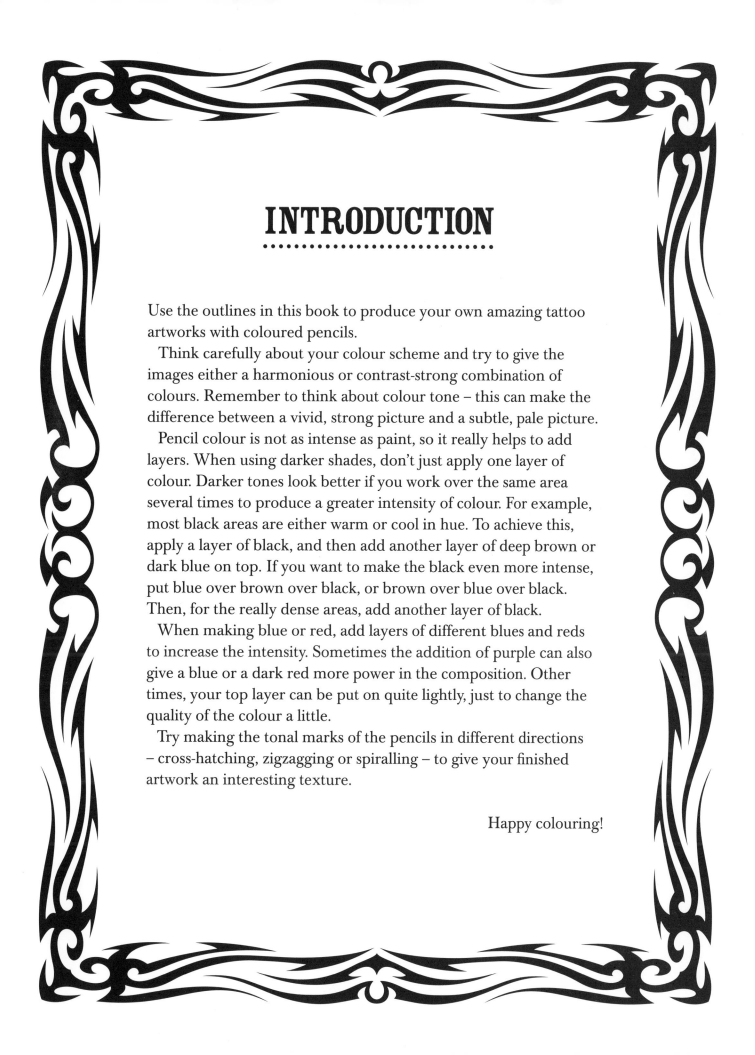

INTRODUCTION

Use the outlines in this book to produce your own amazing tattoo artworks with coloured pencils.

Think carefully about your colour scheme and try to give the images either a harmonious or contrast-strong combination of colours. Remember to think about colour tone – this can make the difference between a vivid, strong picture and a subtle, pale picture.

Pencil colour is not as intense as paint, so it really helps to add layers. When using darker shades, don't just apply one layer of colour. Darker tones look better if you work over the same area several times to produce a greater intensity of colour. For example, most black areas are either warm or cool in hue. To achieve this, apply a layer of black, and then add another layer of deep brown or dark blue on top. If you want to make the black even more intense, put blue over brown over black, or brown over blue over black. Then, for the really dense areas, add another layer of black.

When making blue or red, add layers of different blues and reds to increase the intensity. Sometimes the addition of purple can also give a blue or a dark red more power in the composition. Other times, your top layer can be put on quite lightly, just to change the quality of the colour a little.

Try making the tonal marks of the pencils in different directions – cross-hatching, zigzagging or spiralling – to give your finished artwork an interesting texture.

Happy colouring!

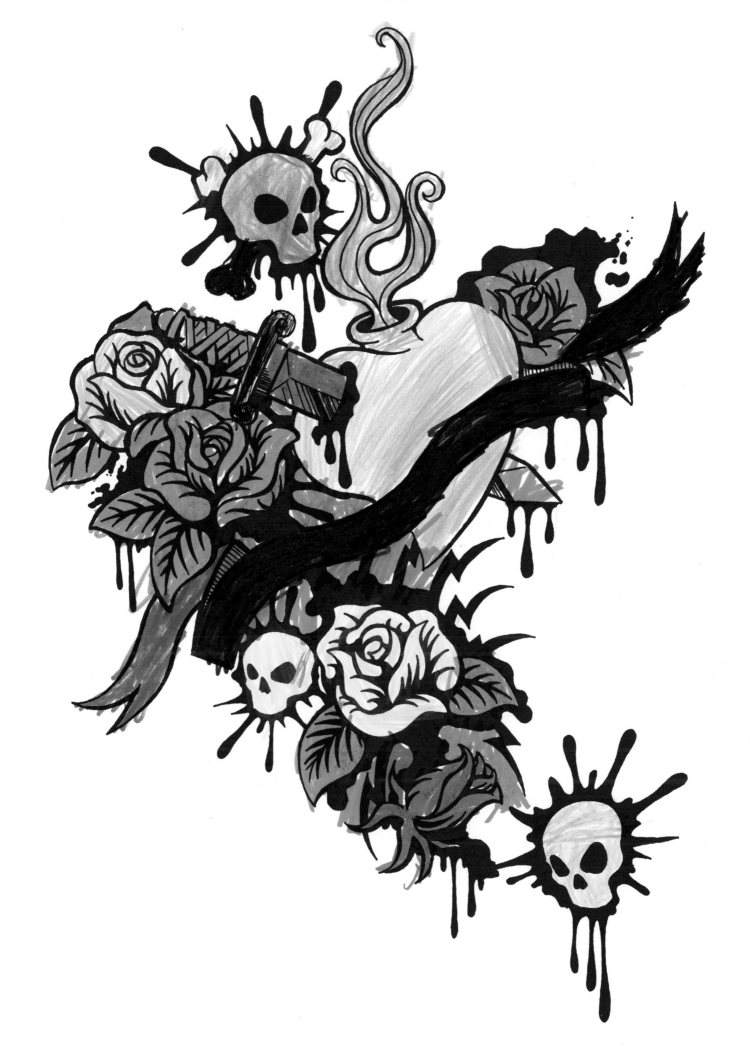

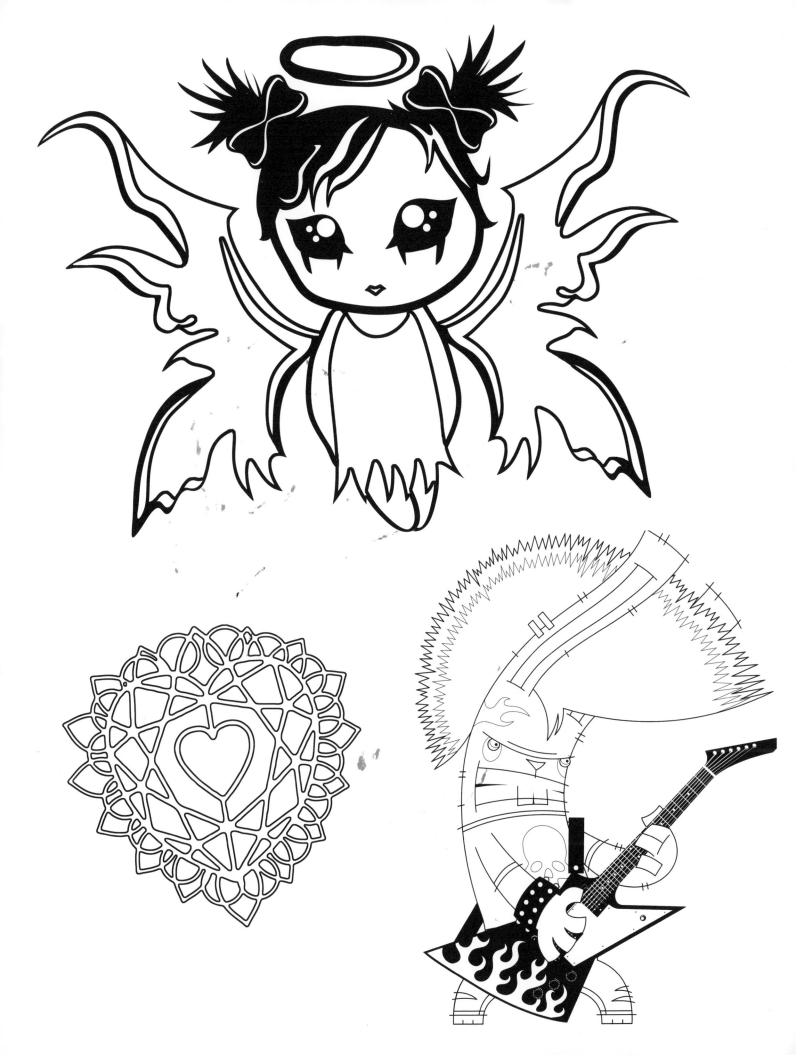

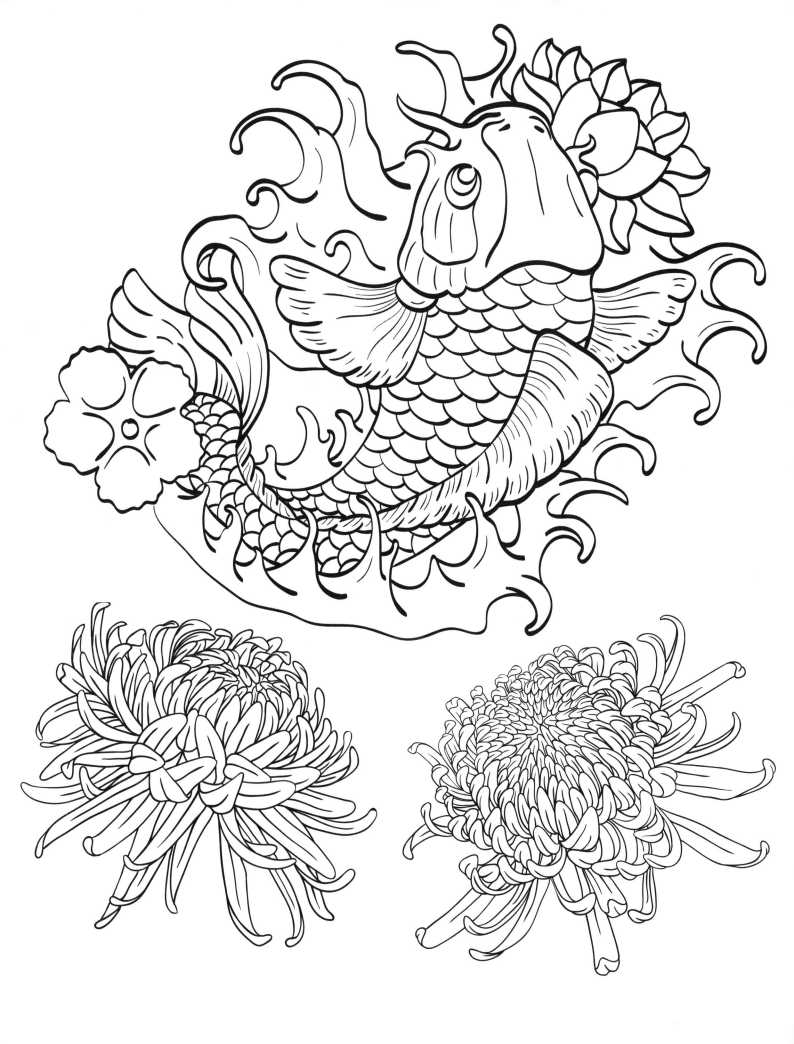

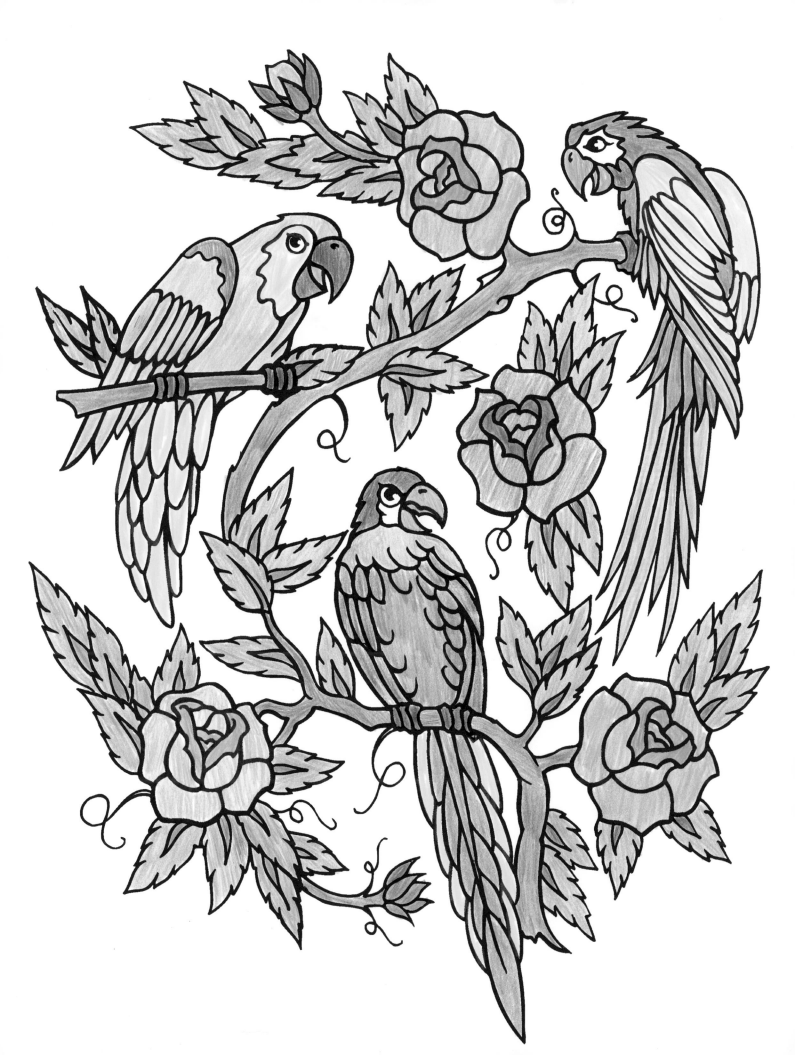

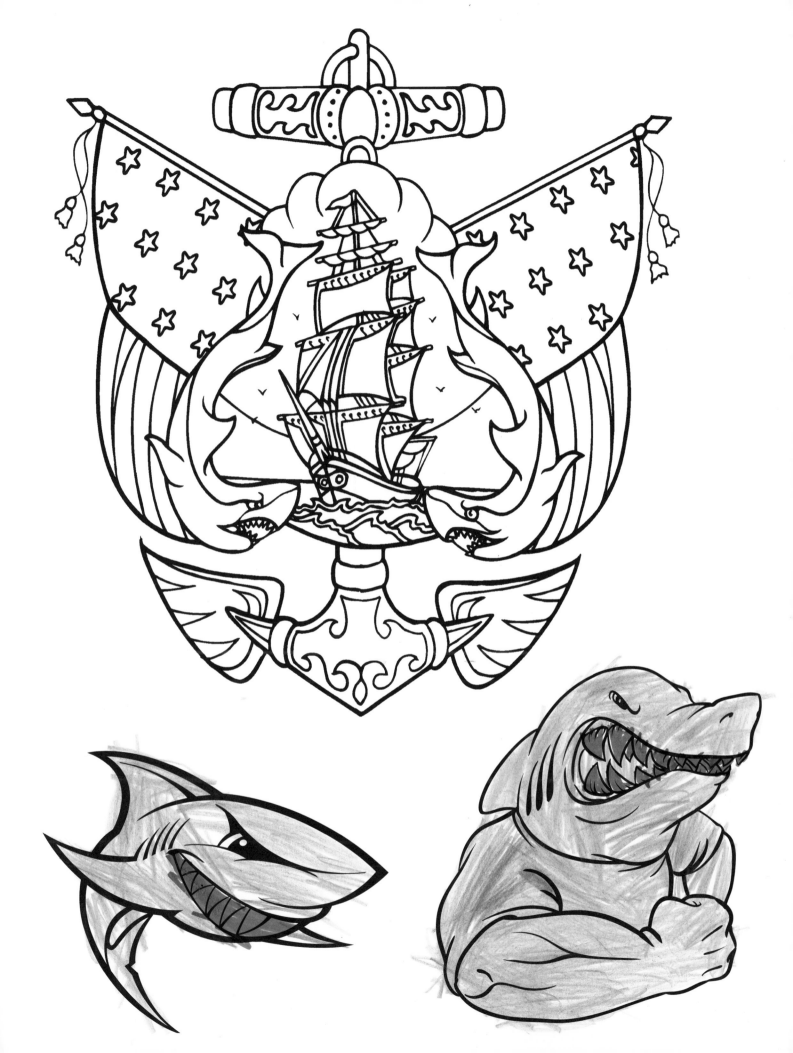

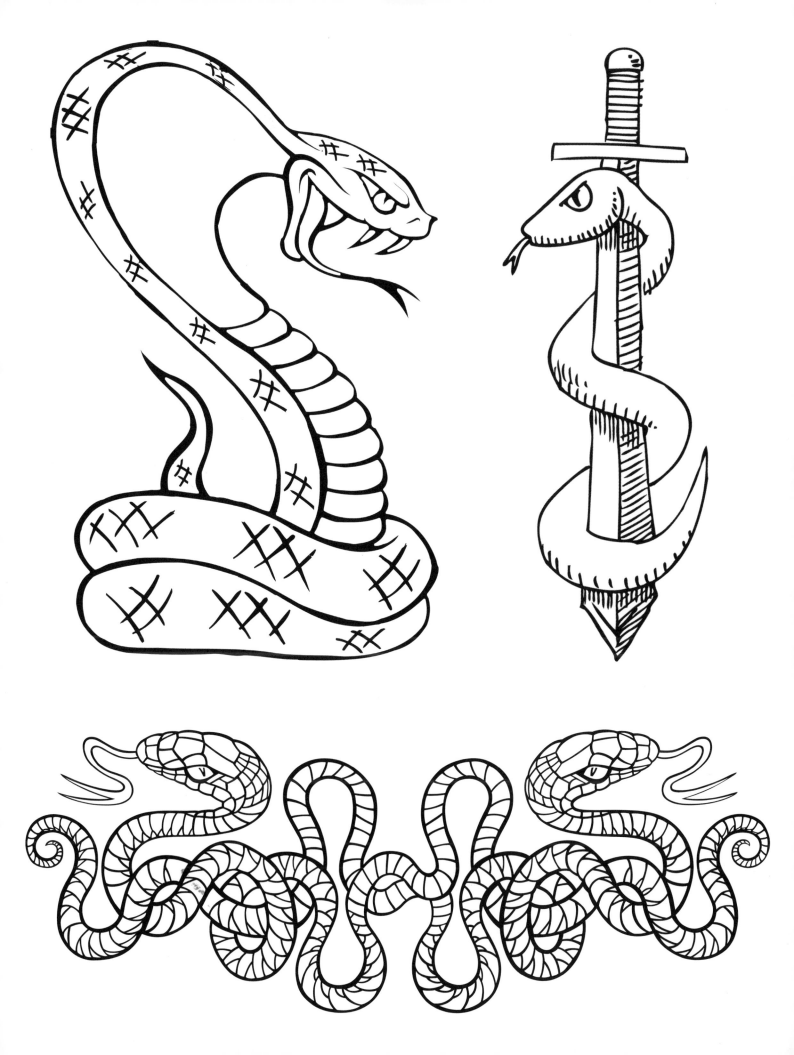

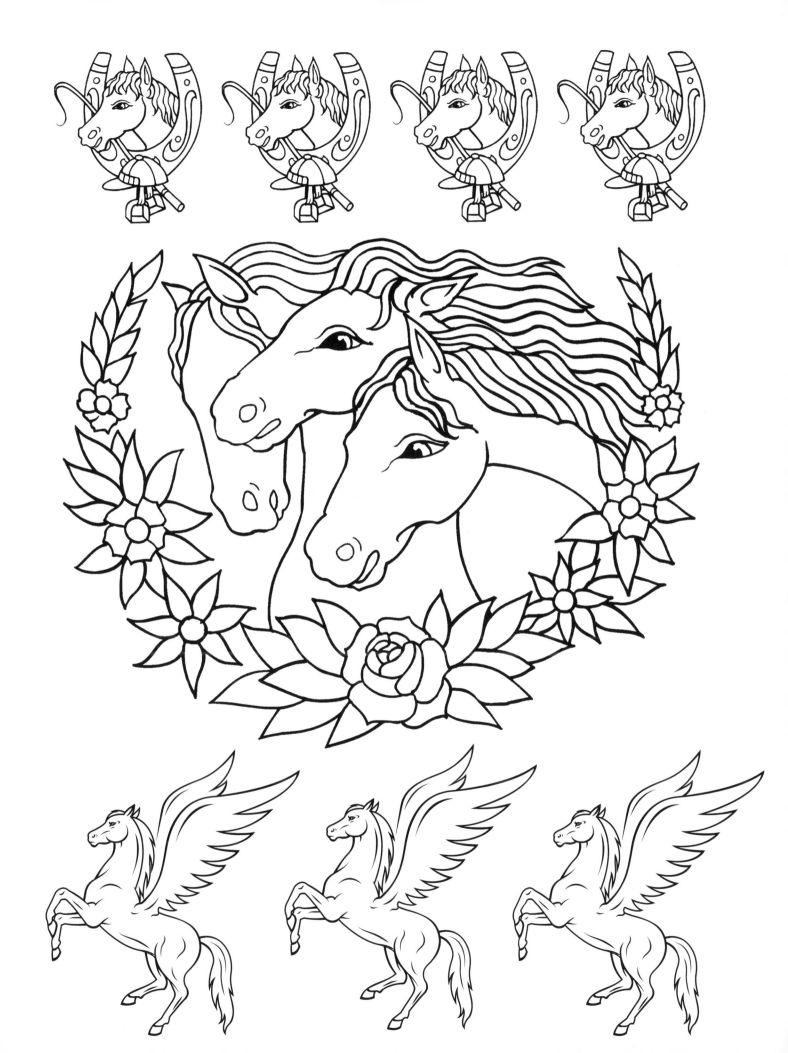

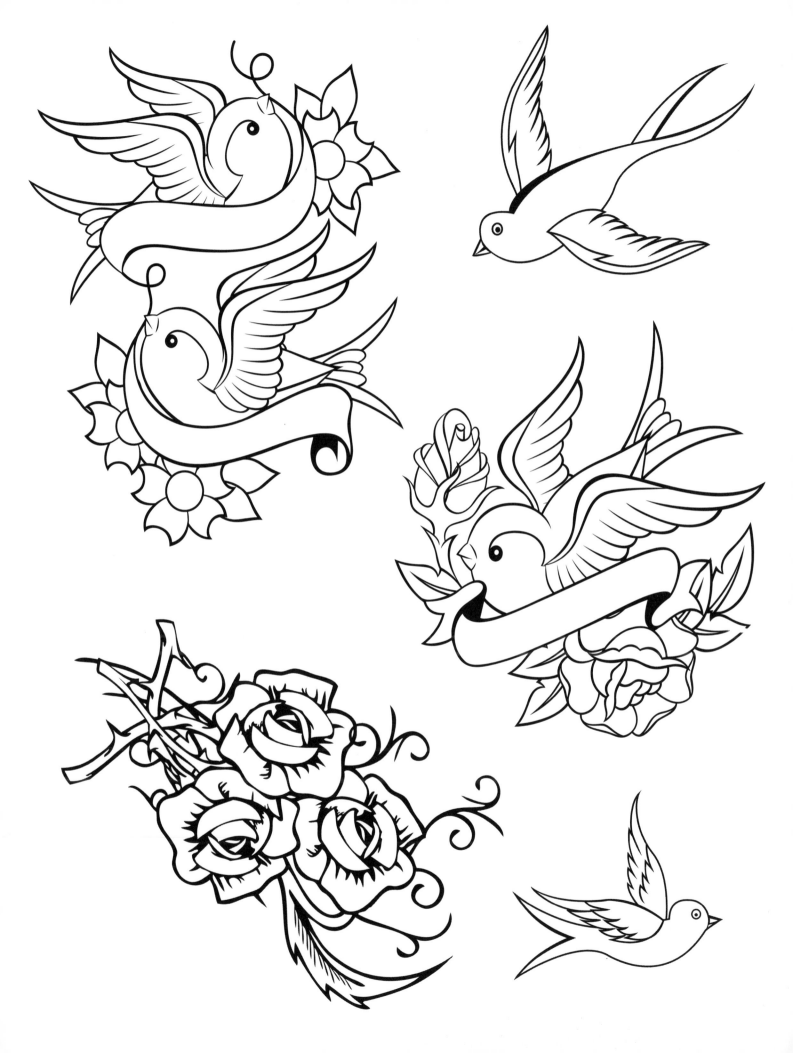

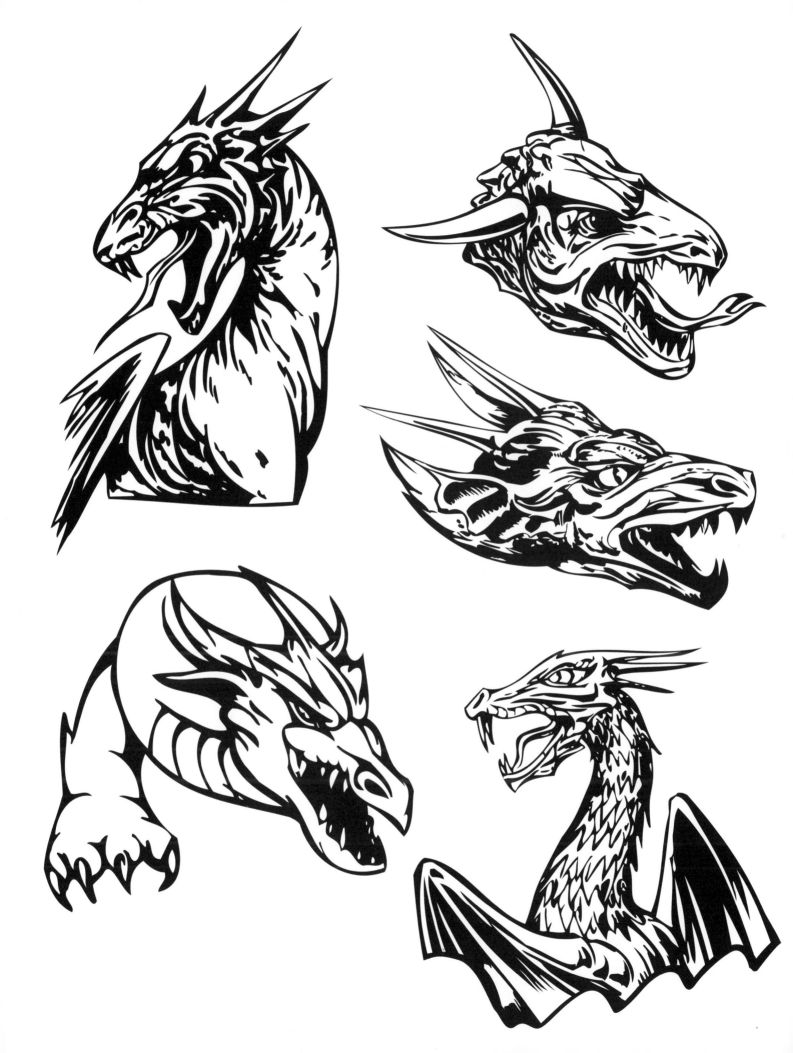

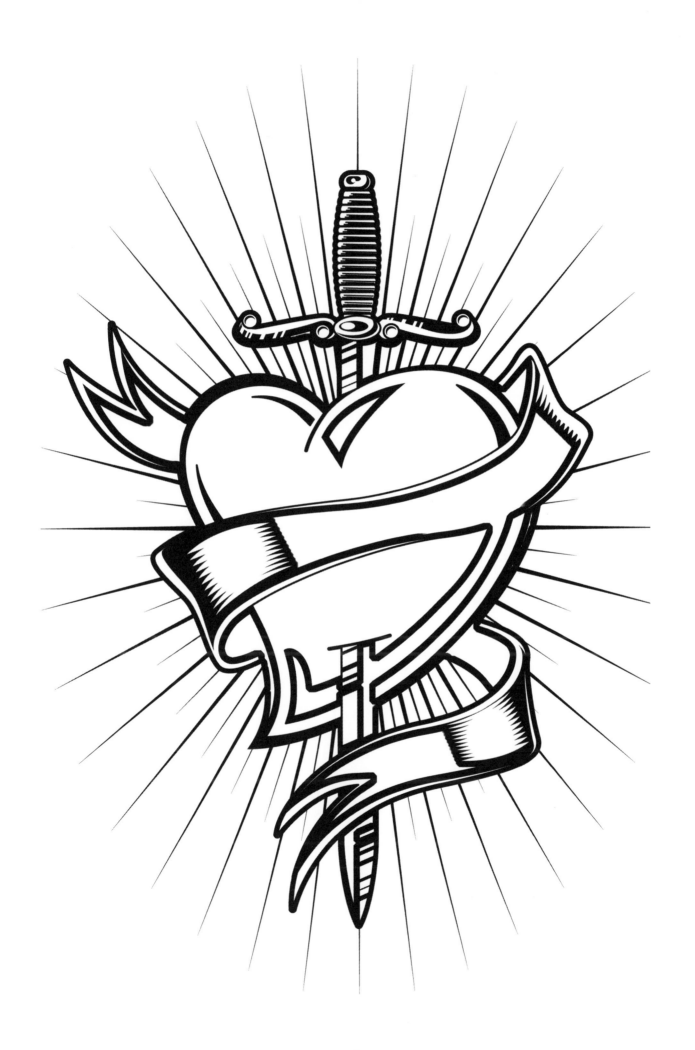

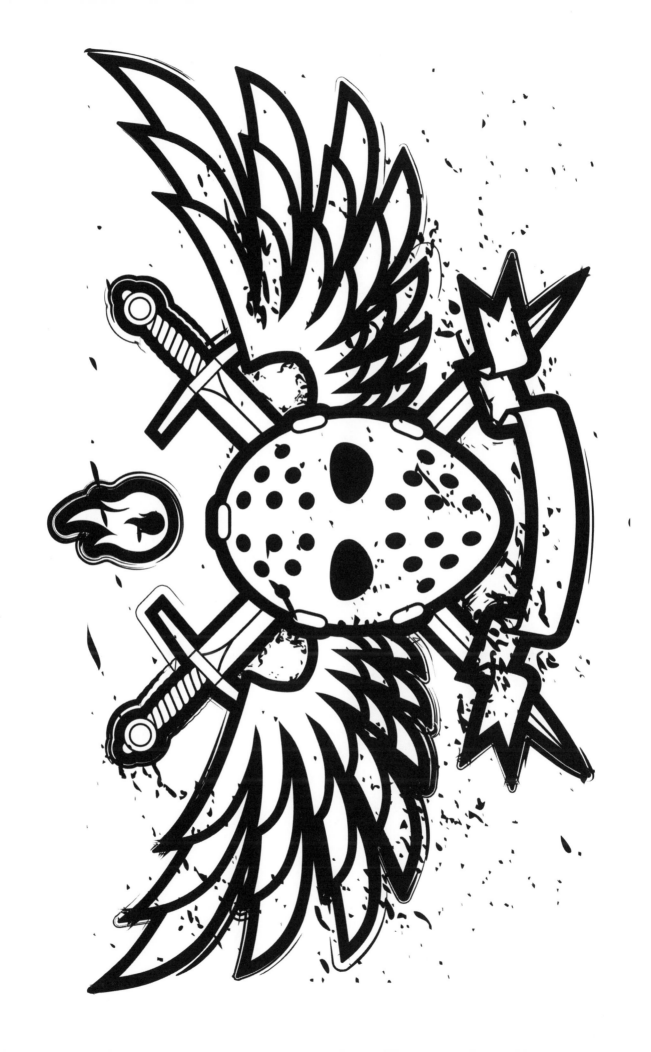

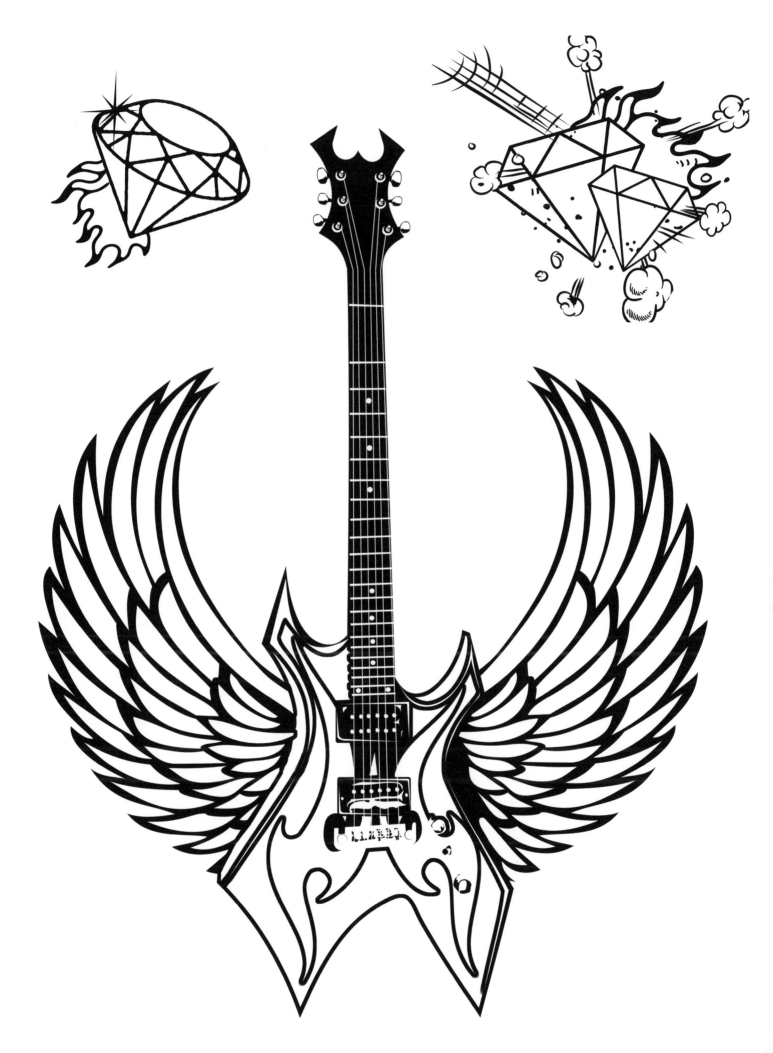

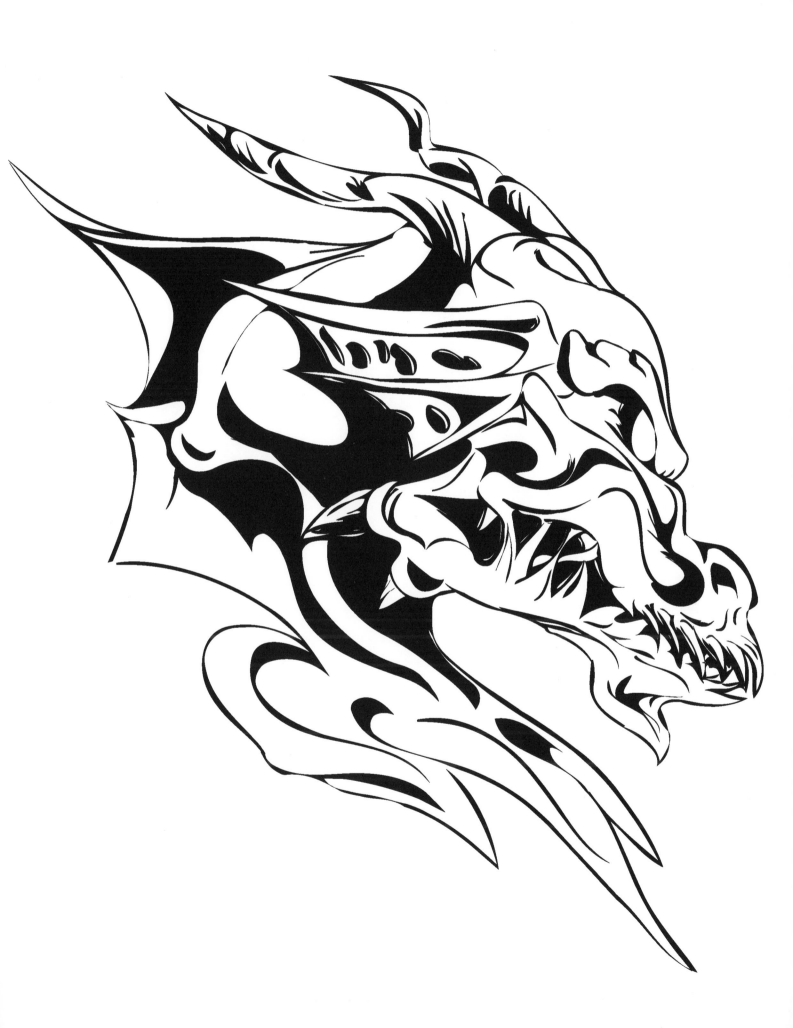

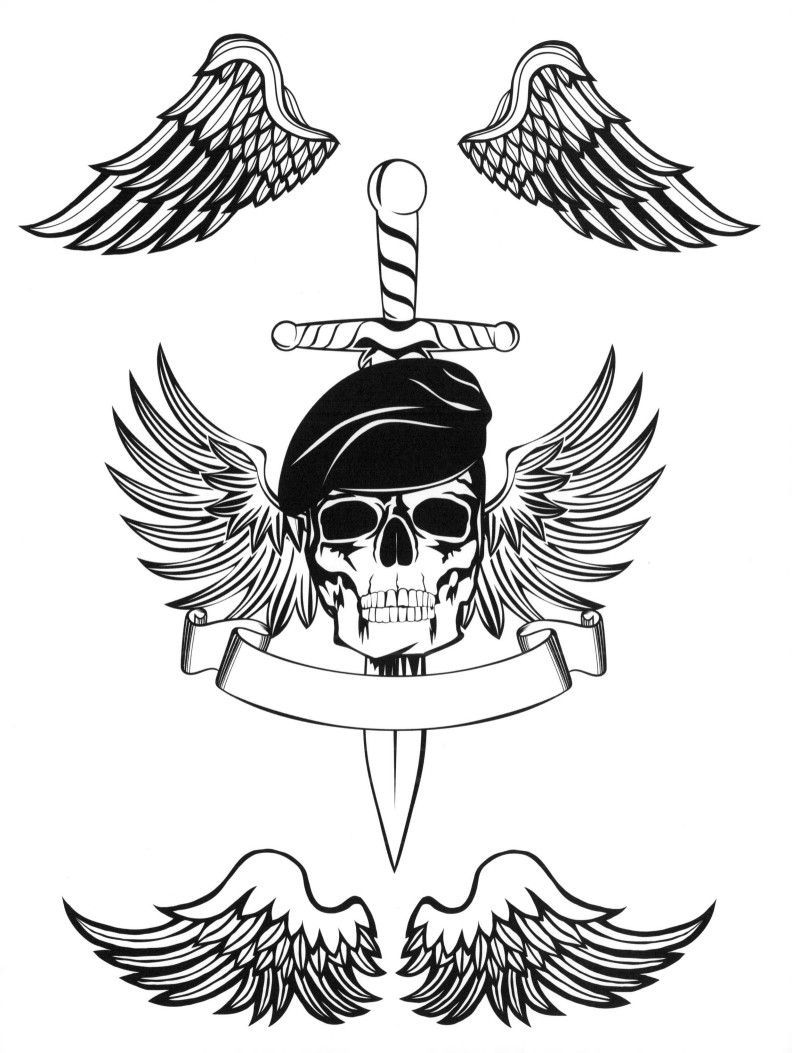

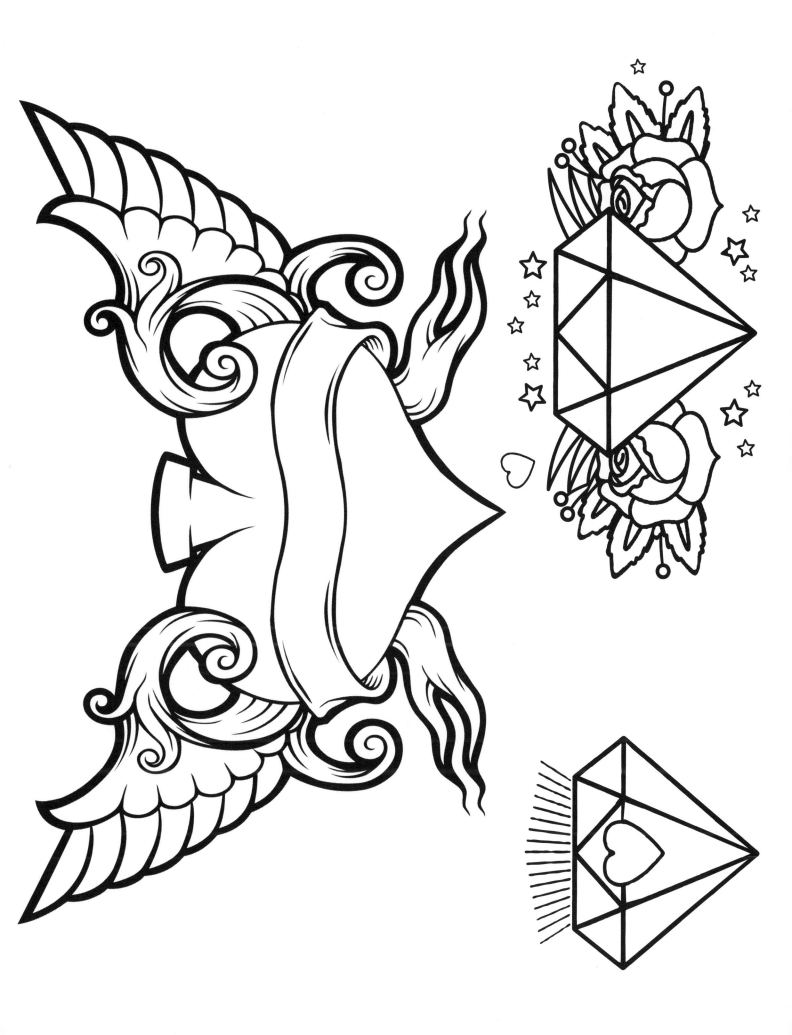

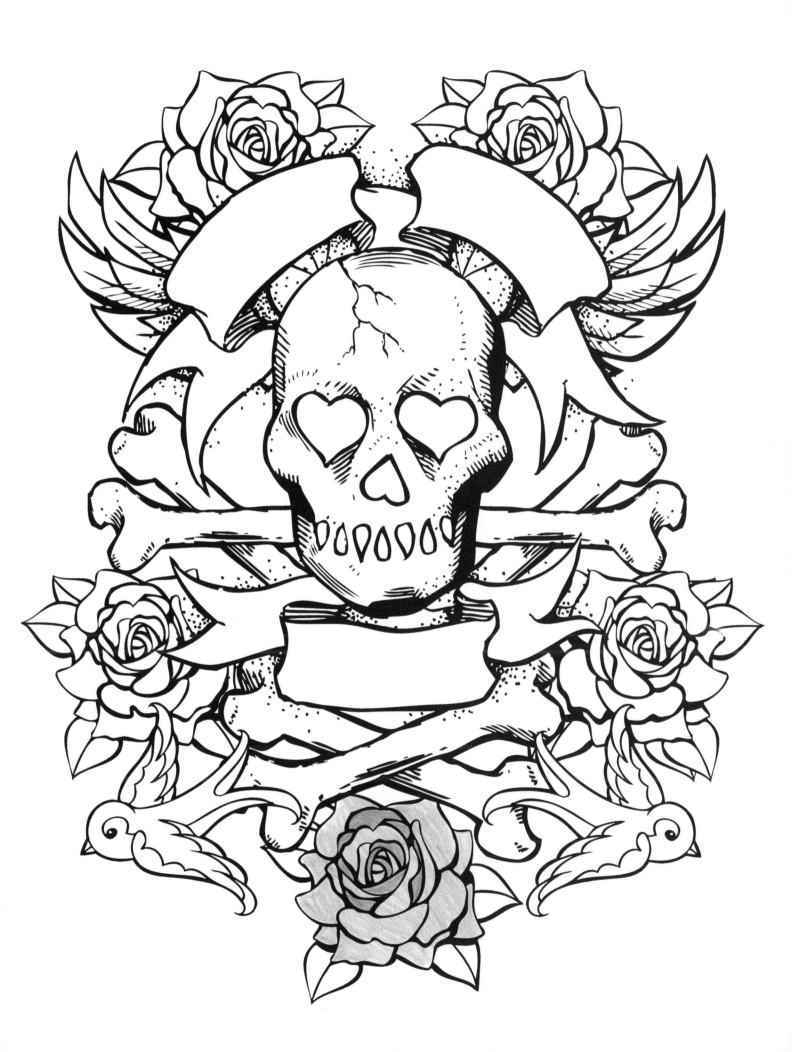

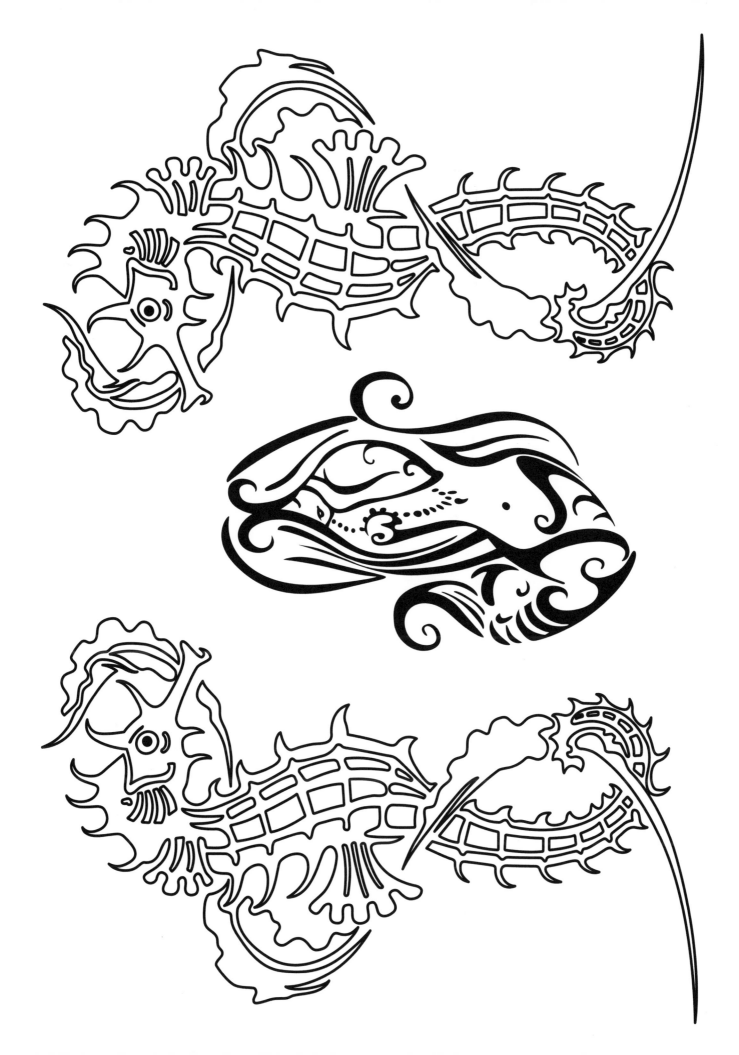

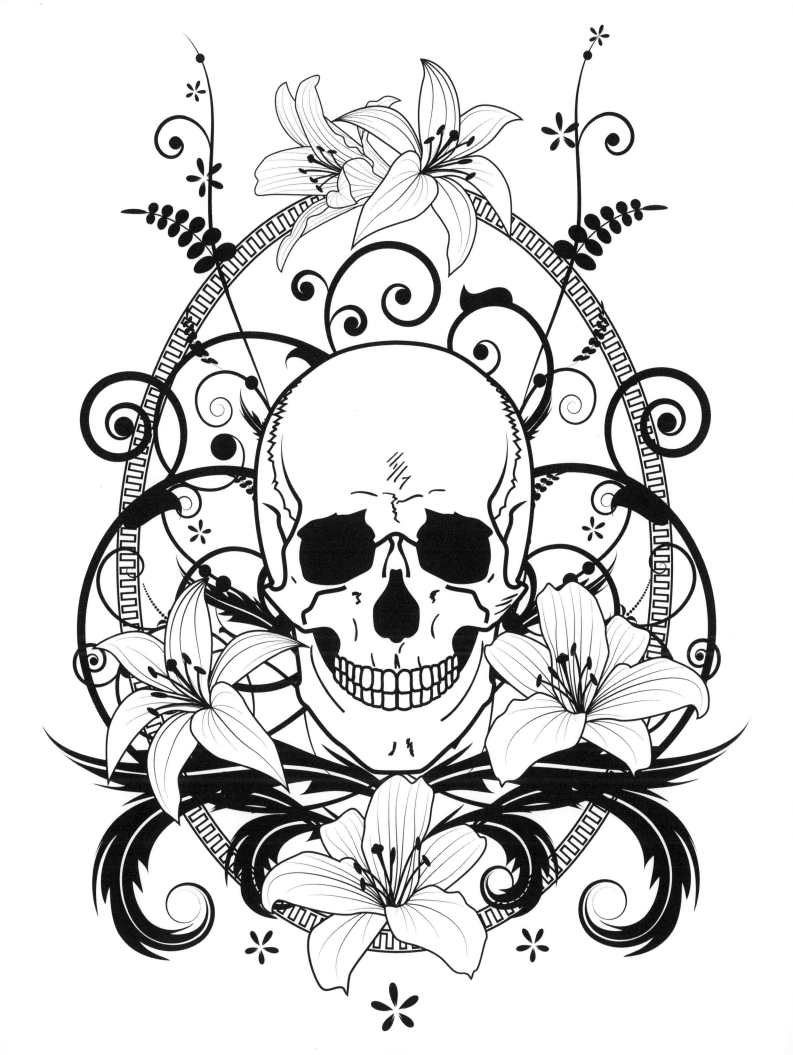

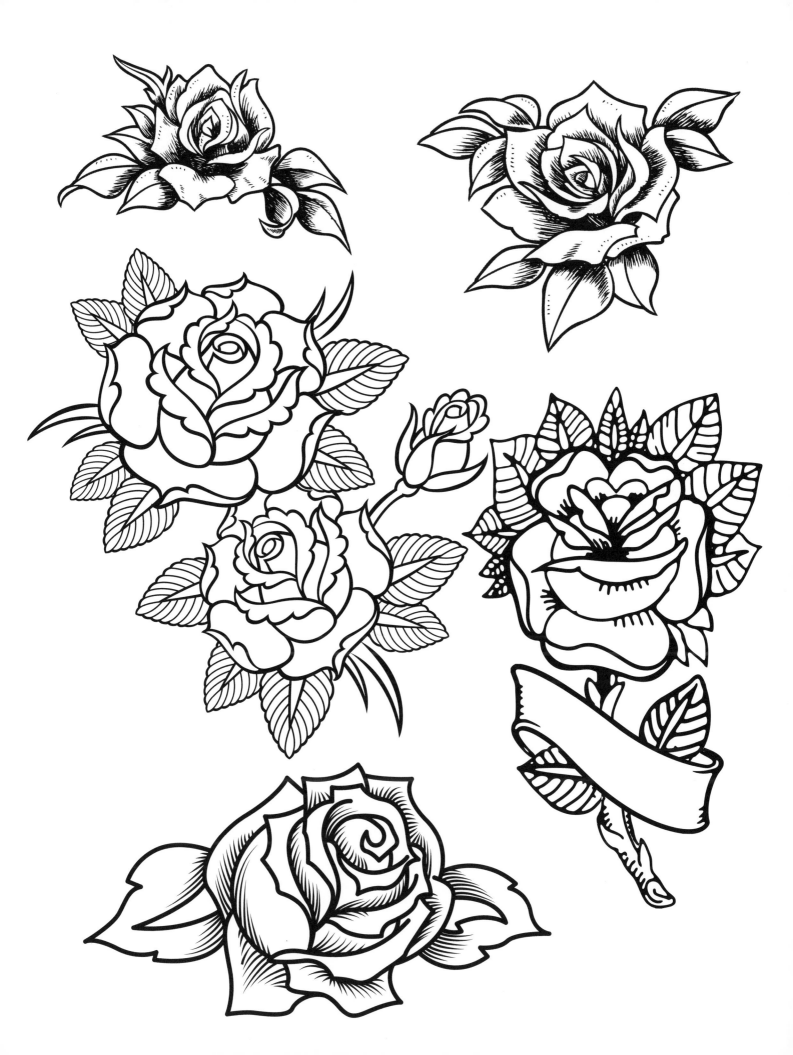

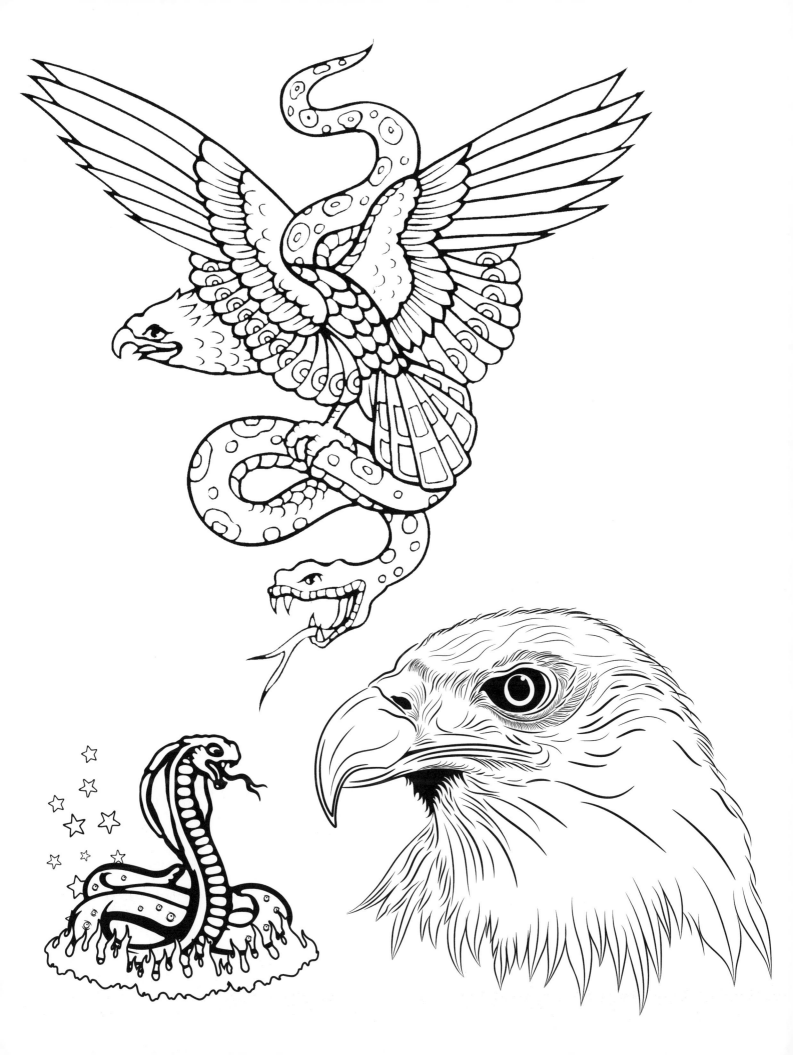

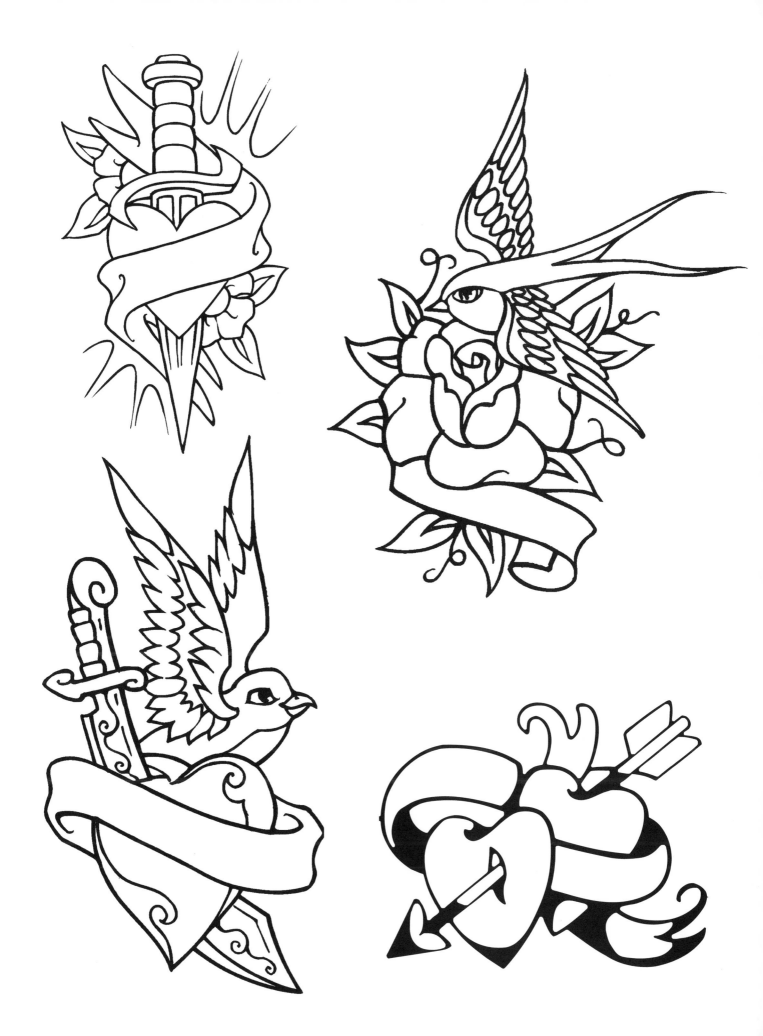

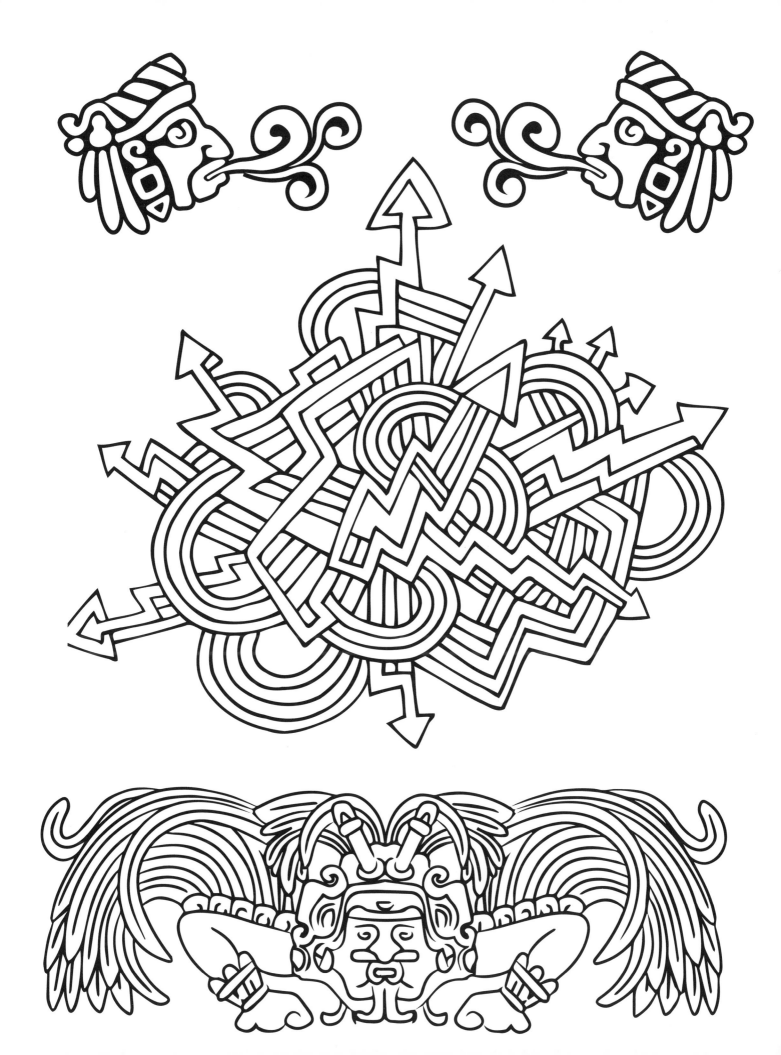

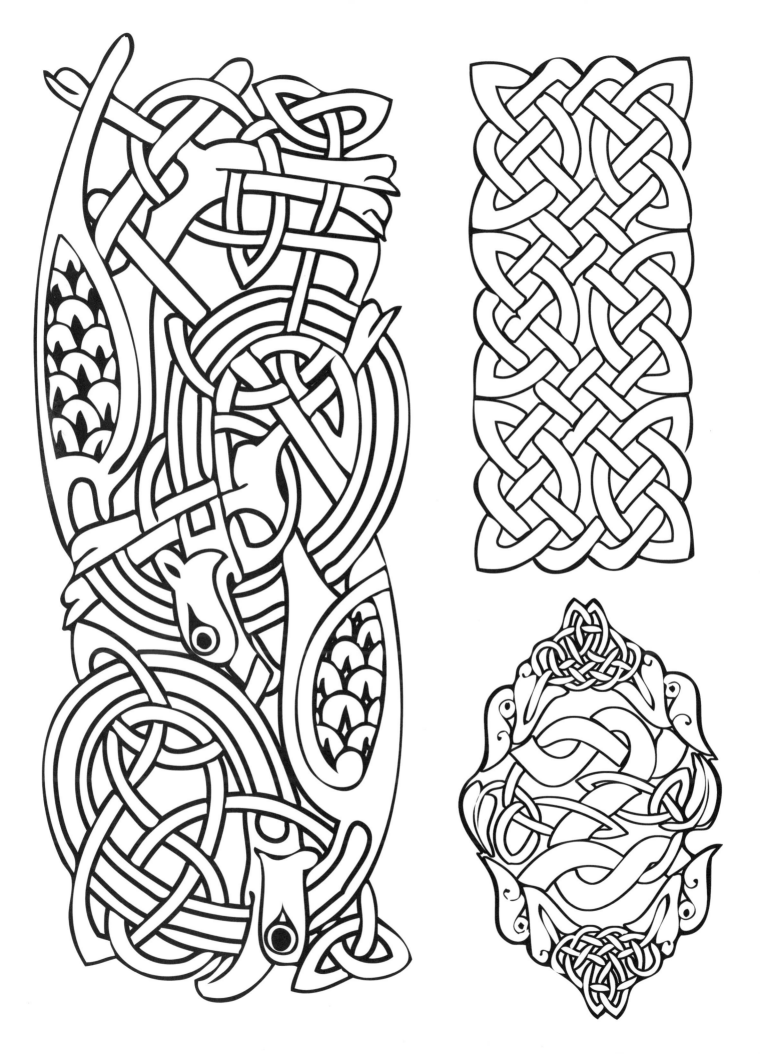

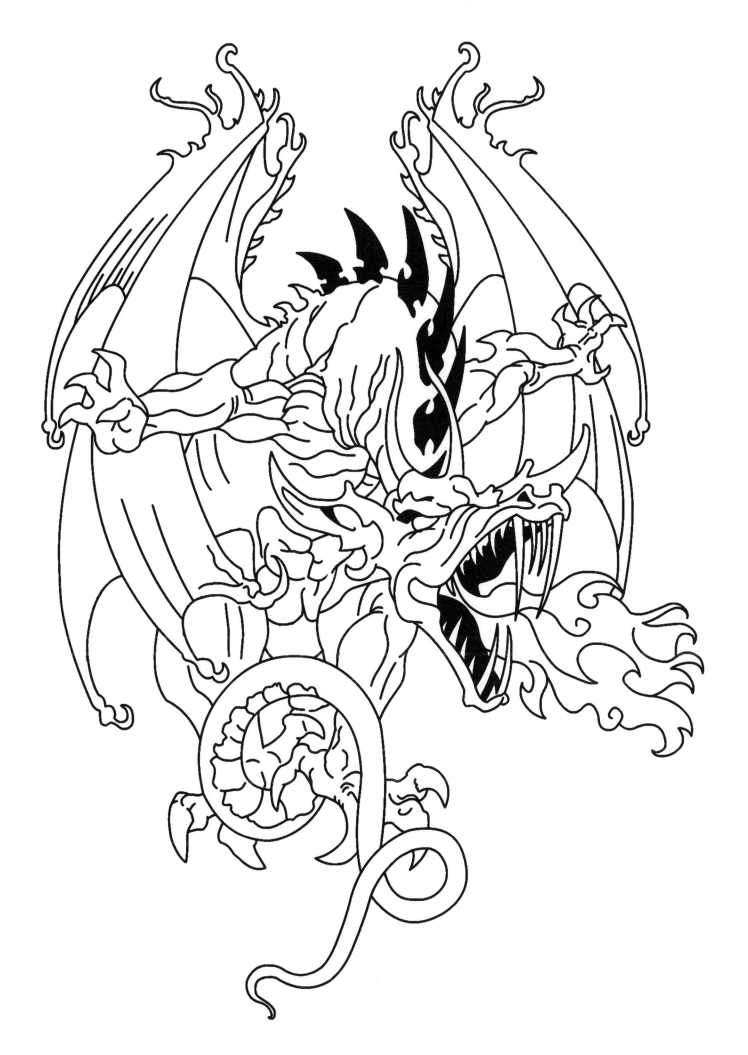

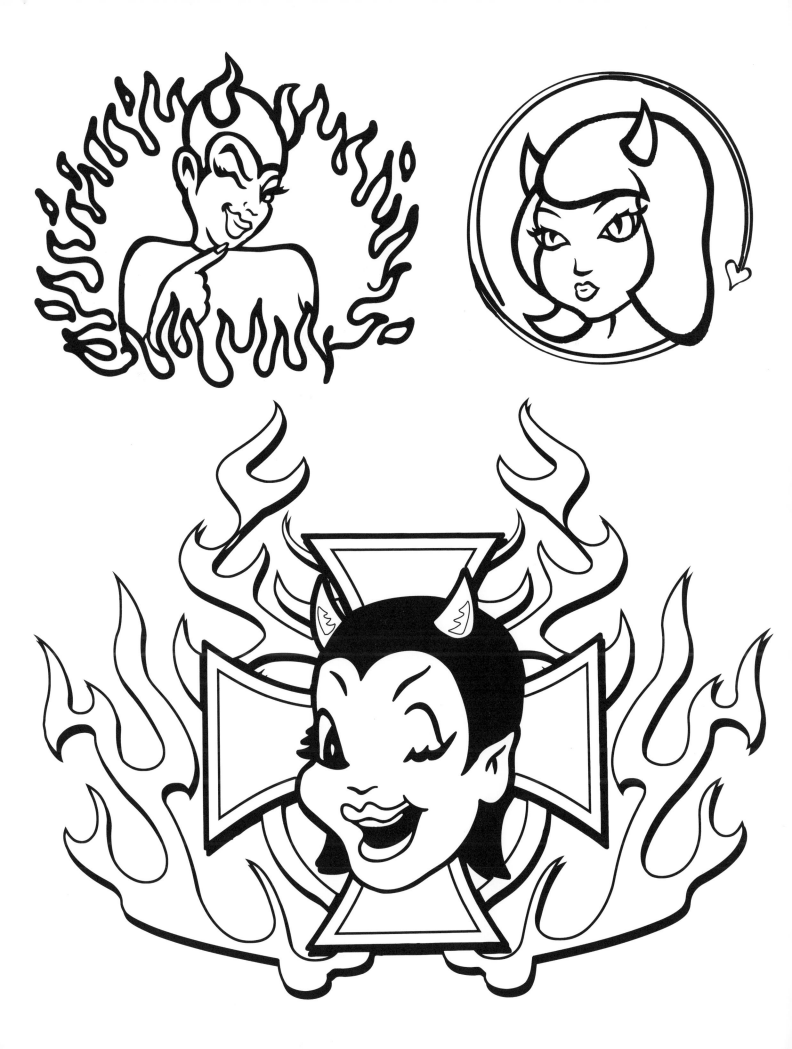

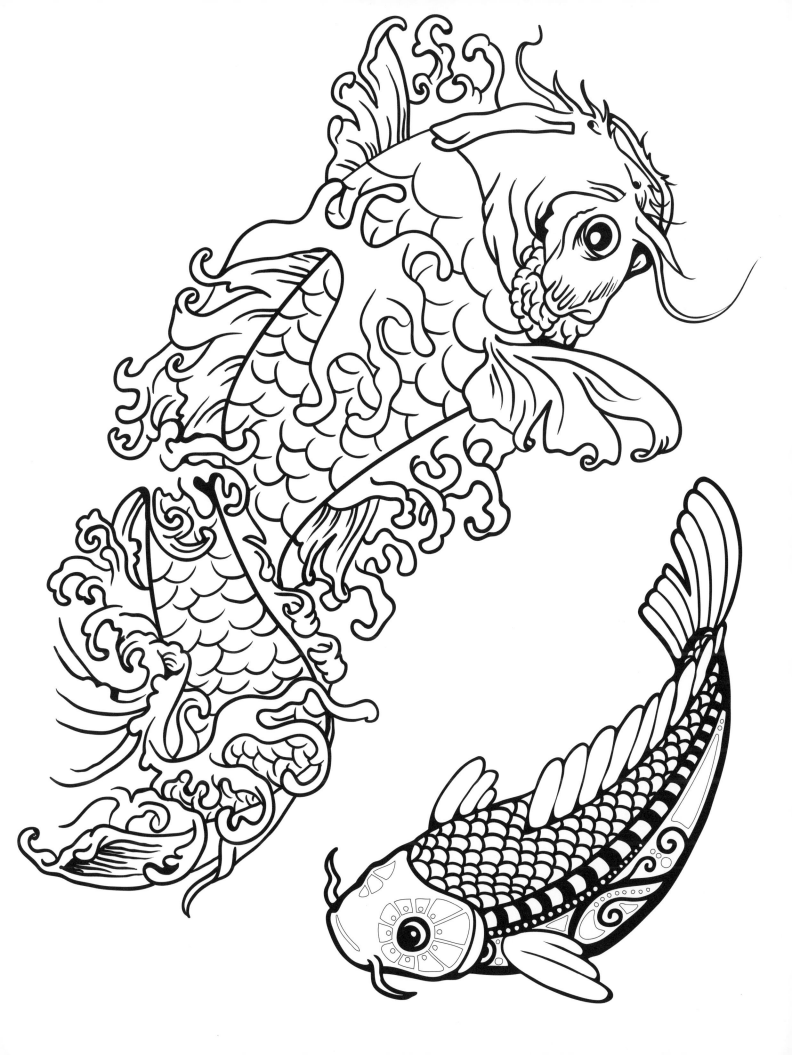

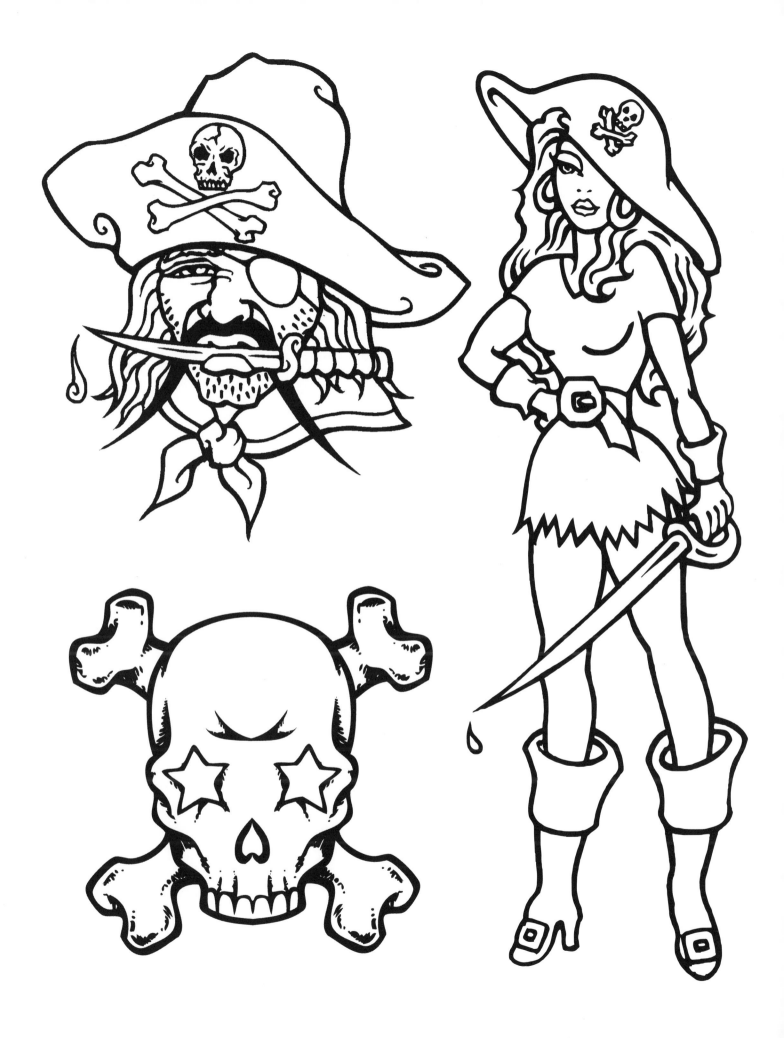

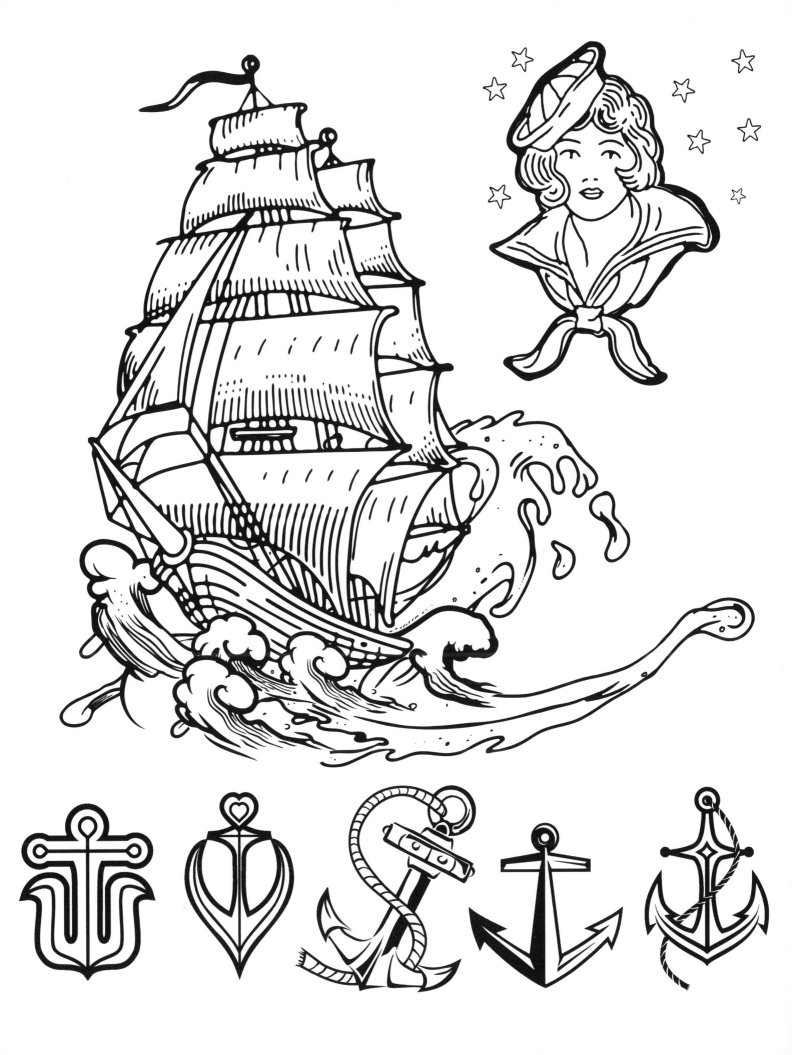

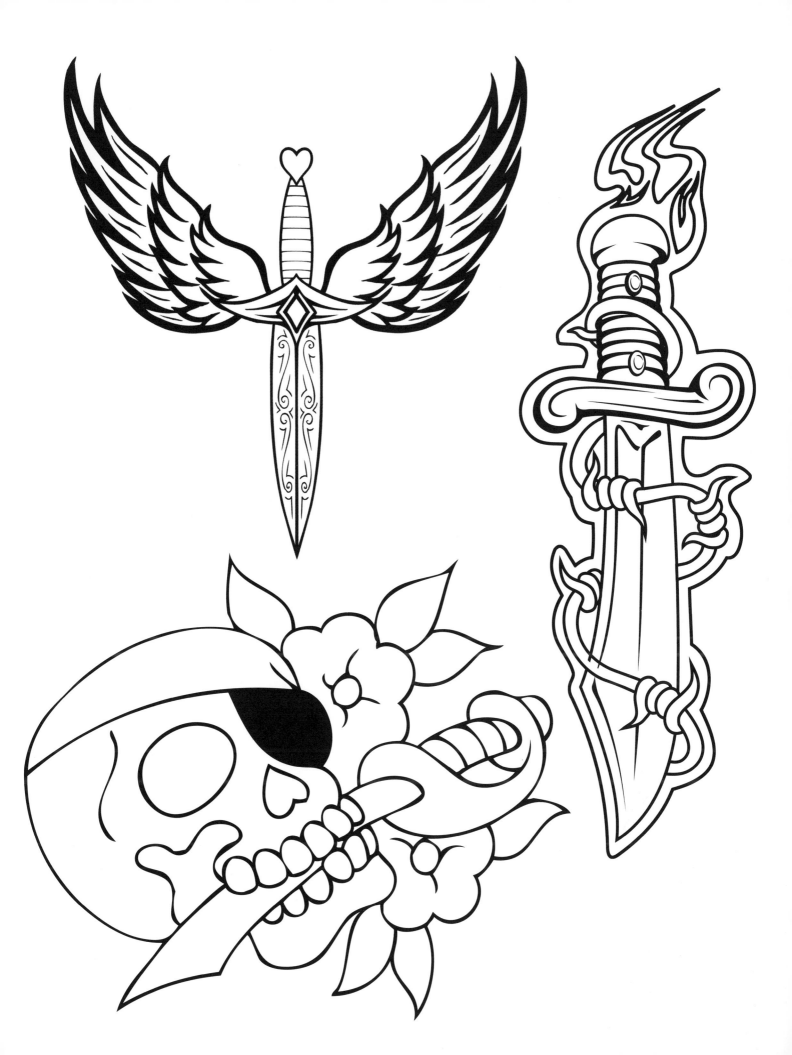

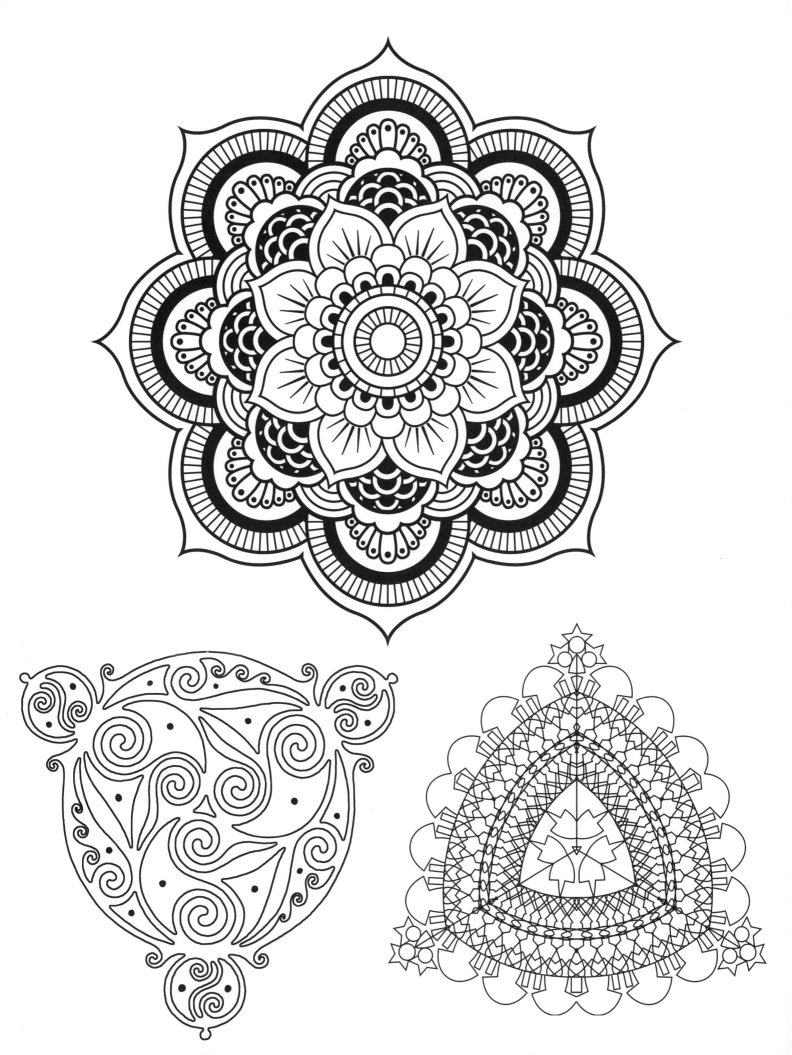

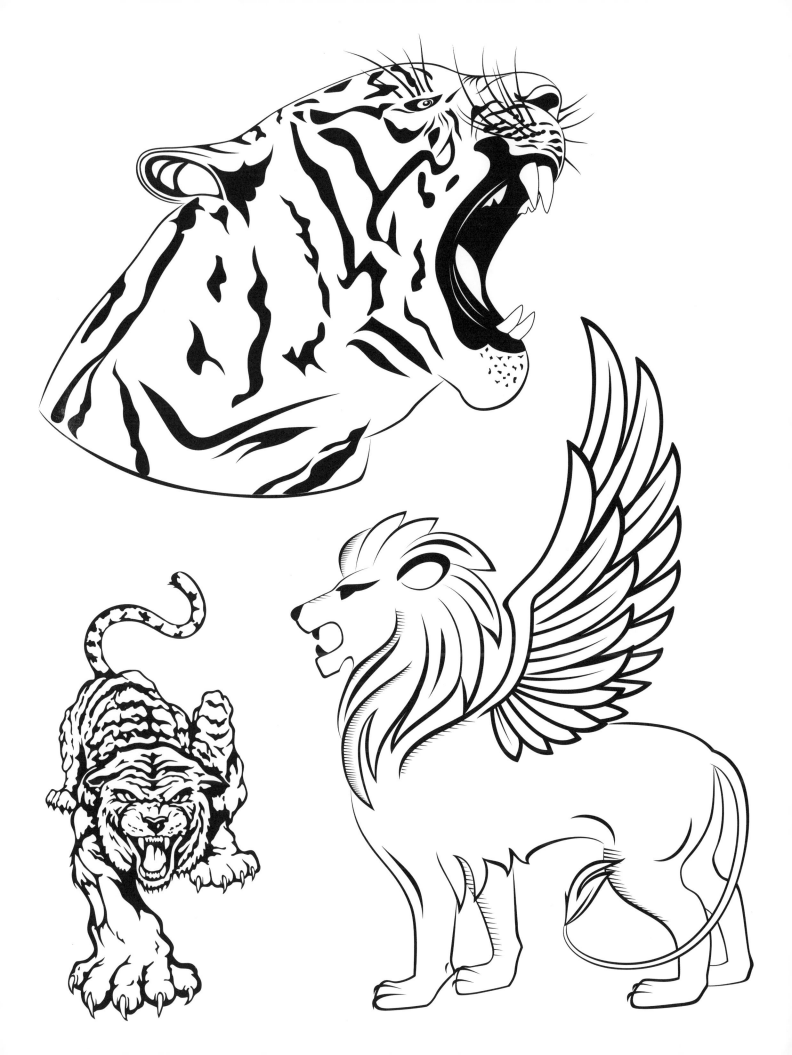

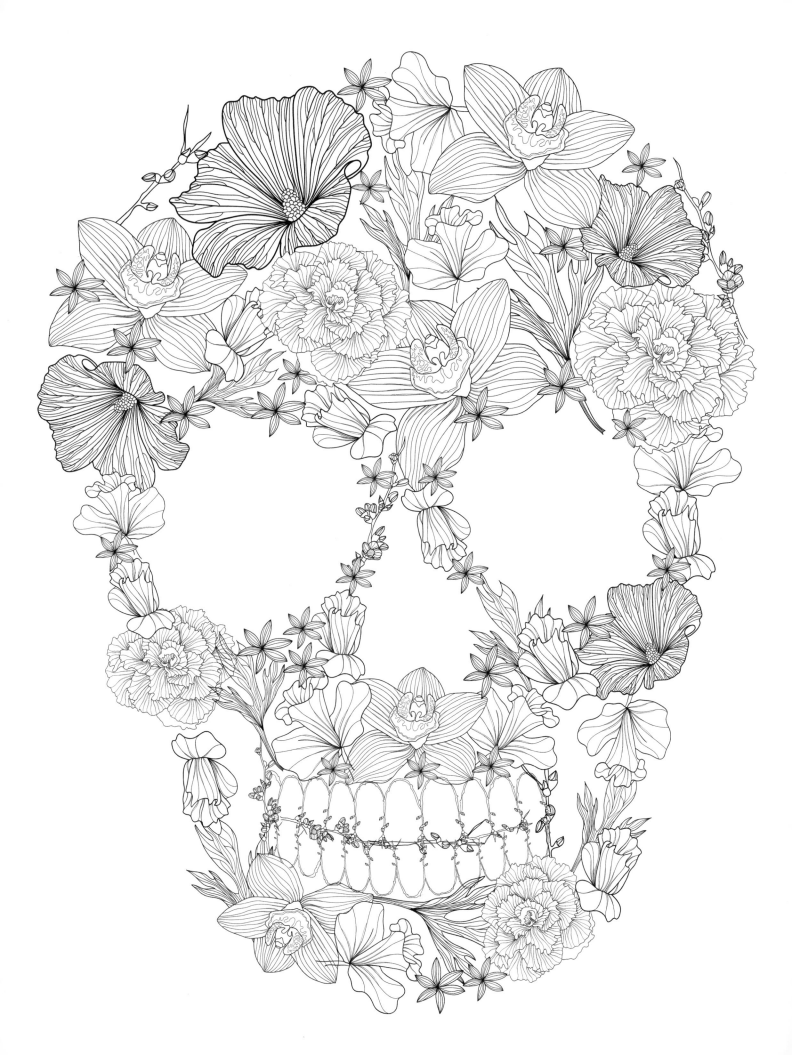

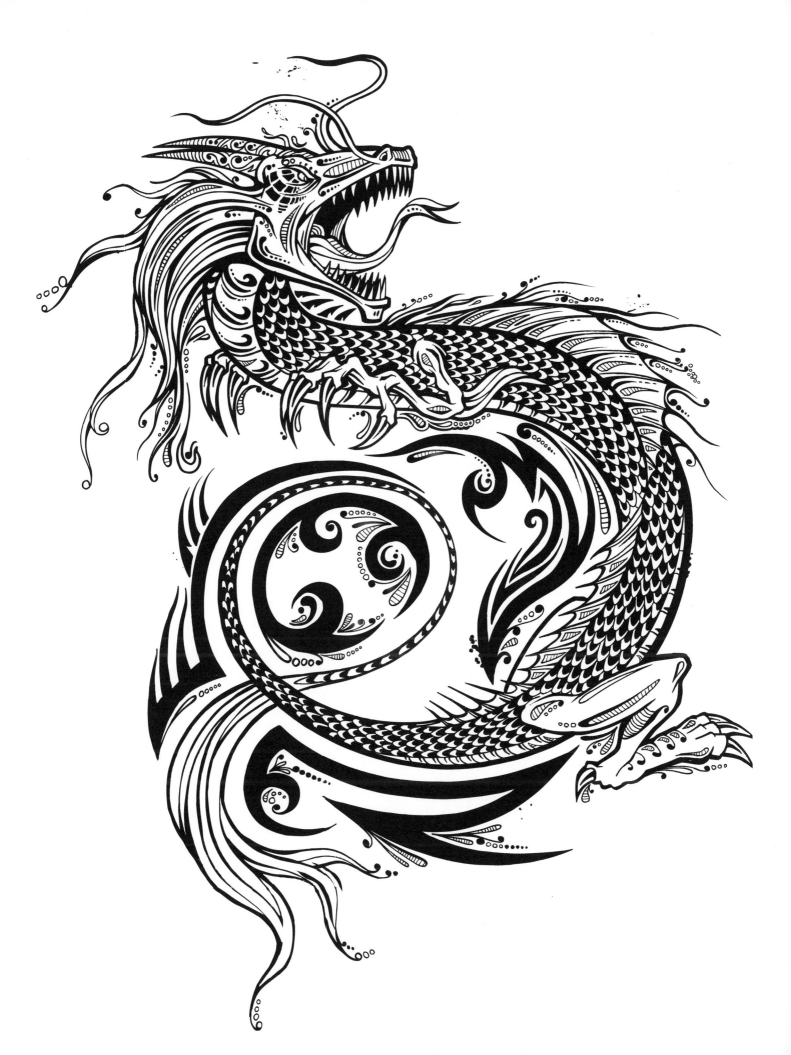

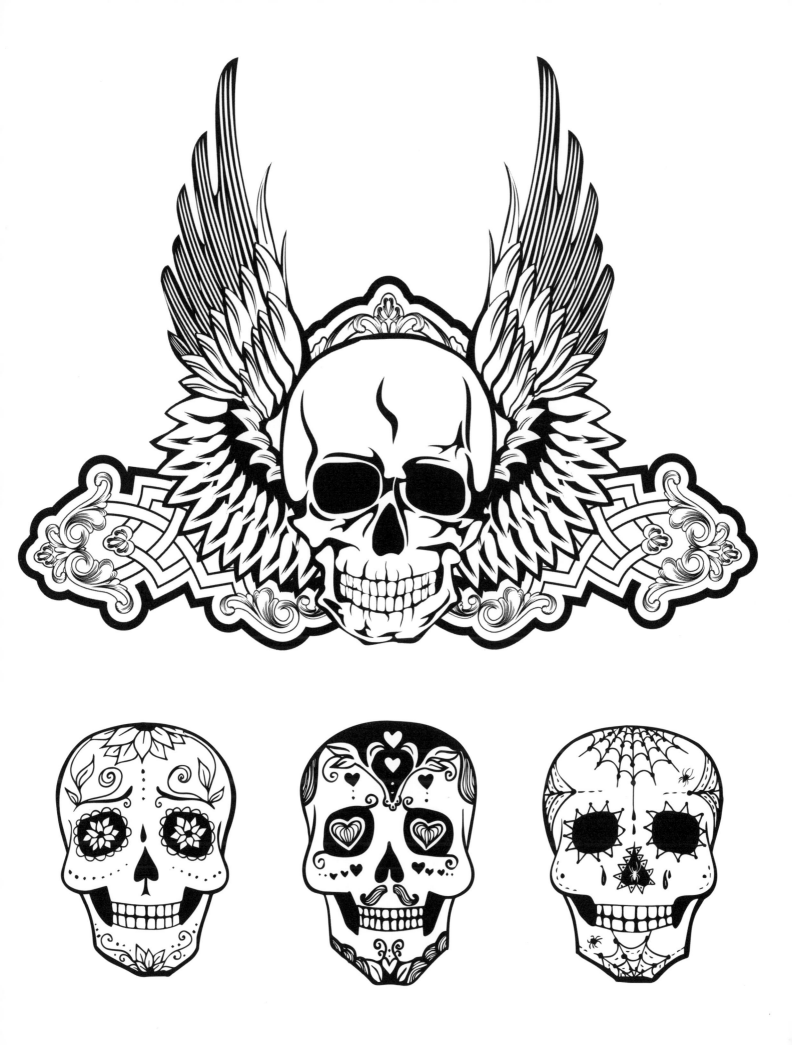

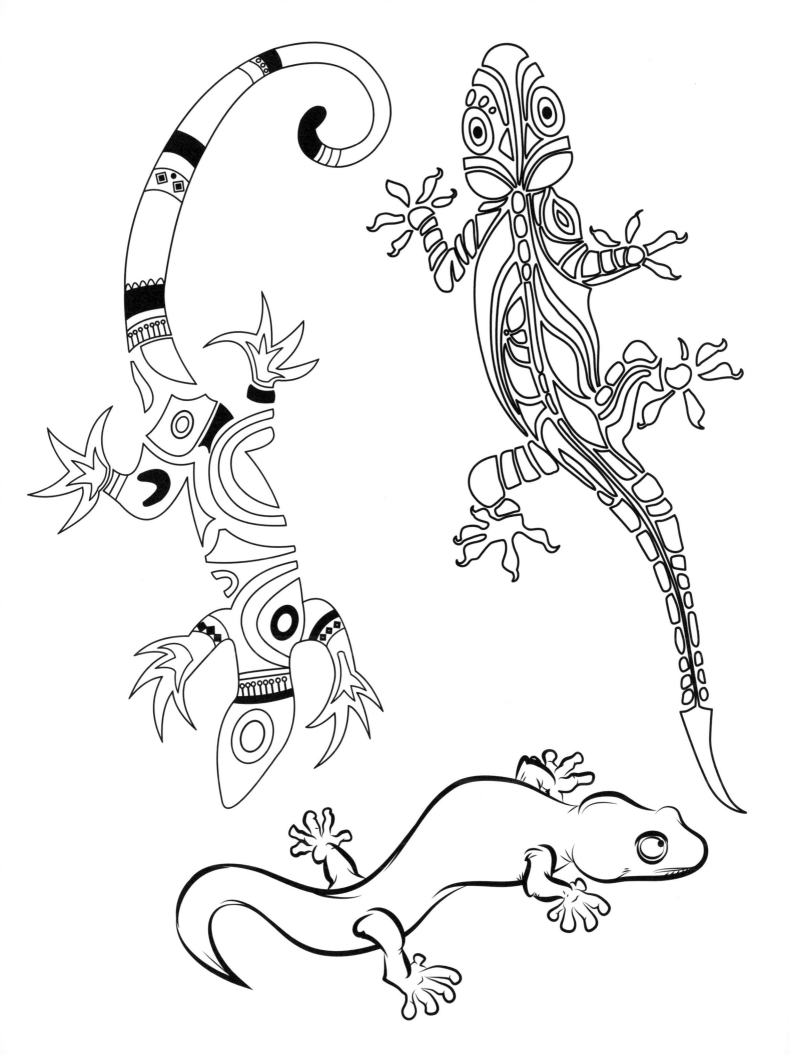

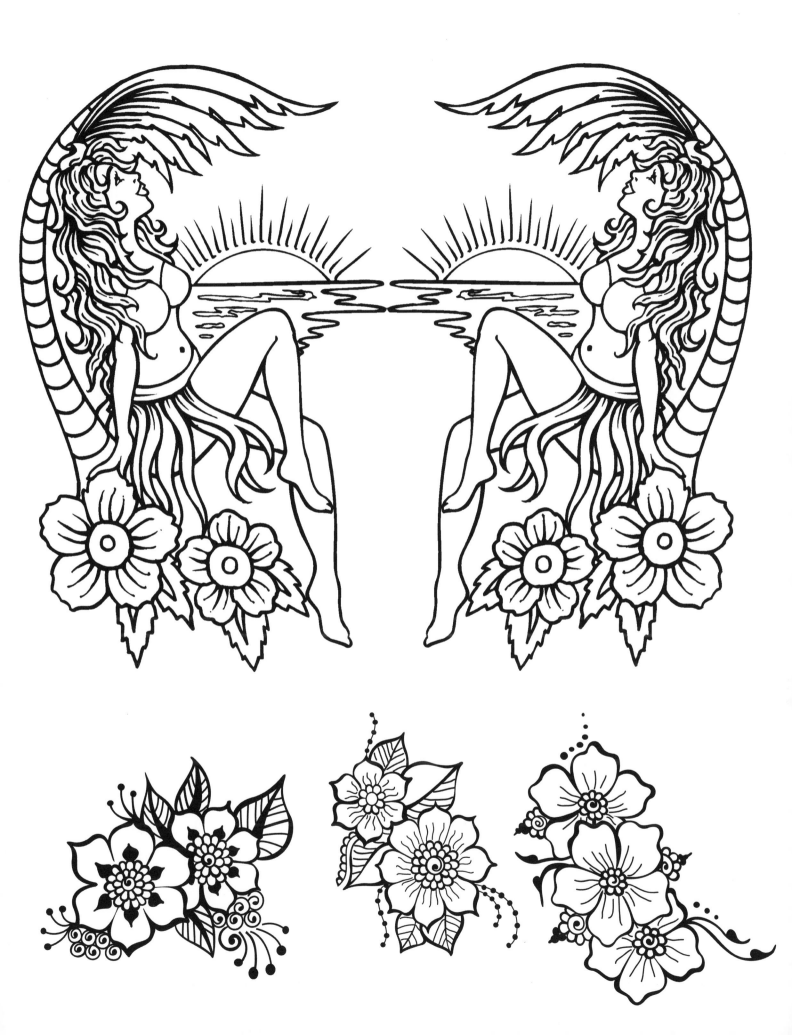

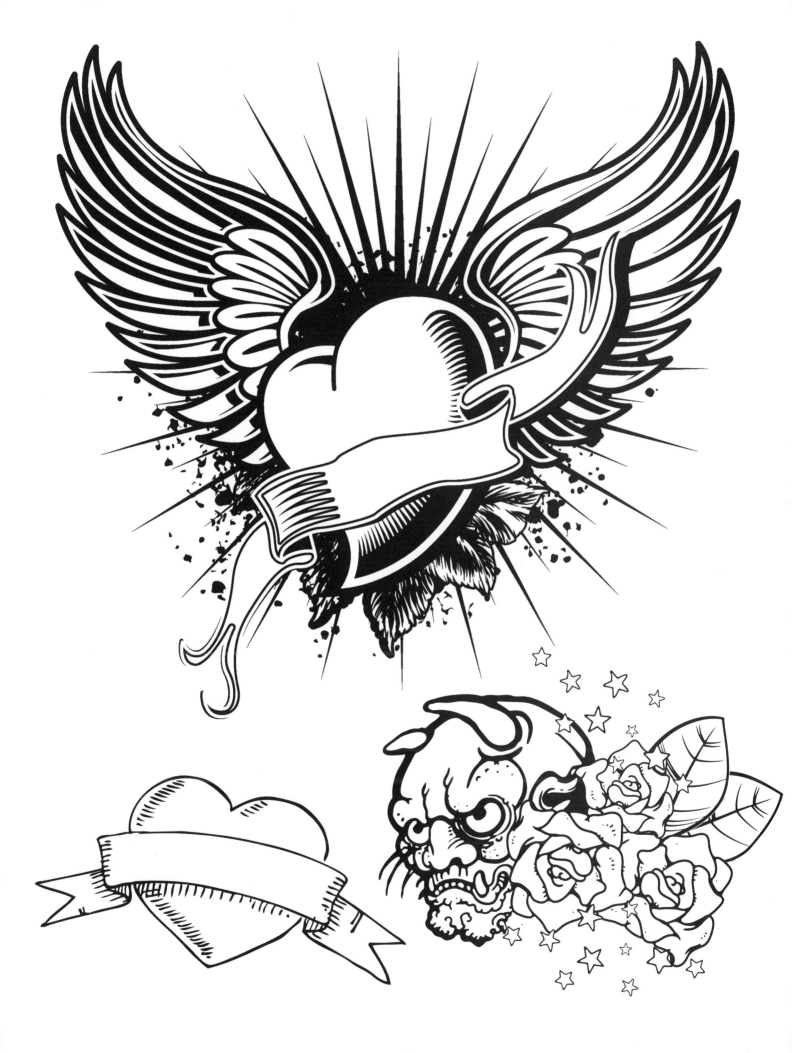

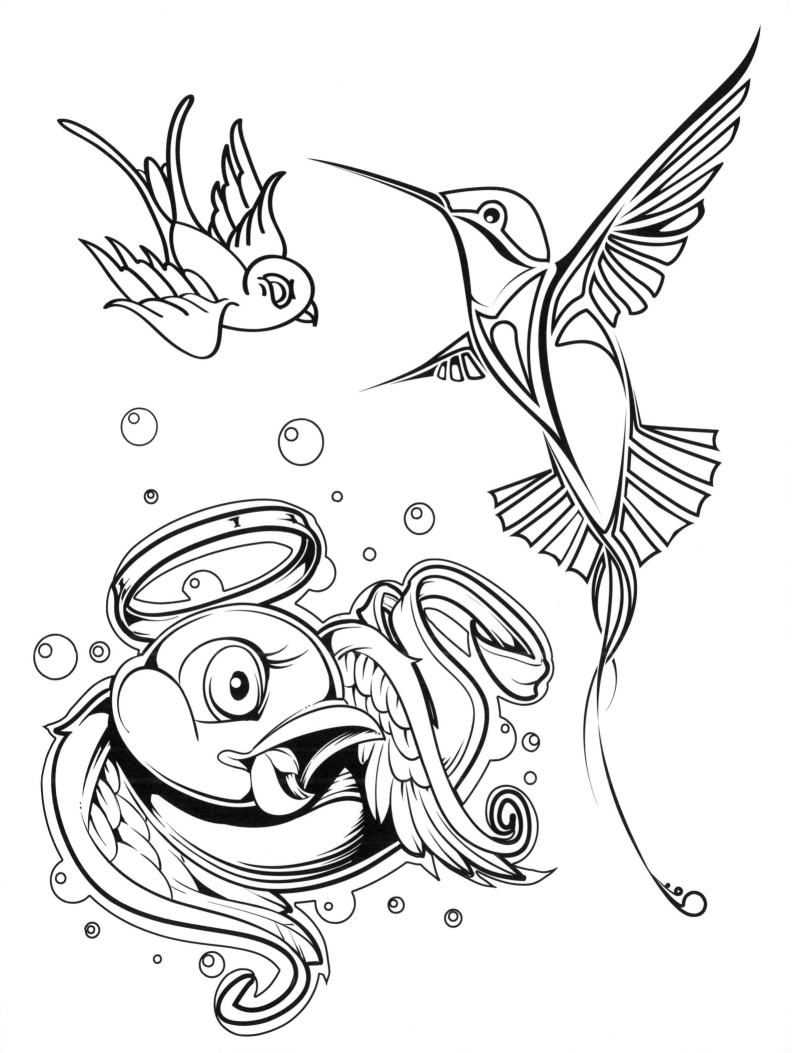

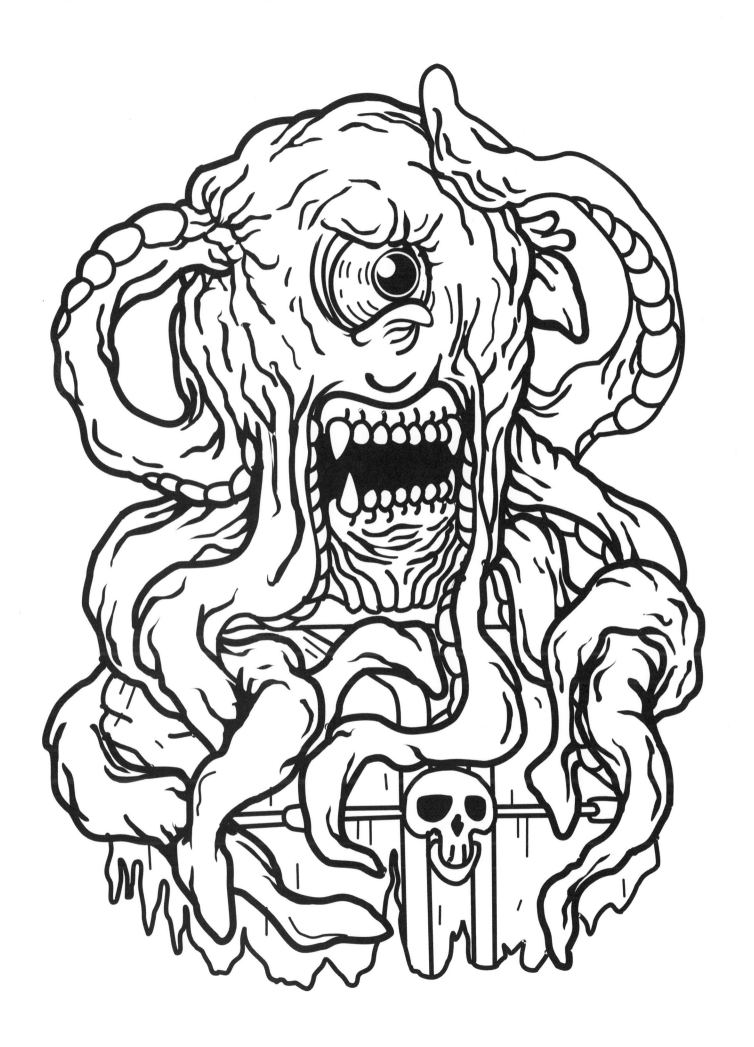

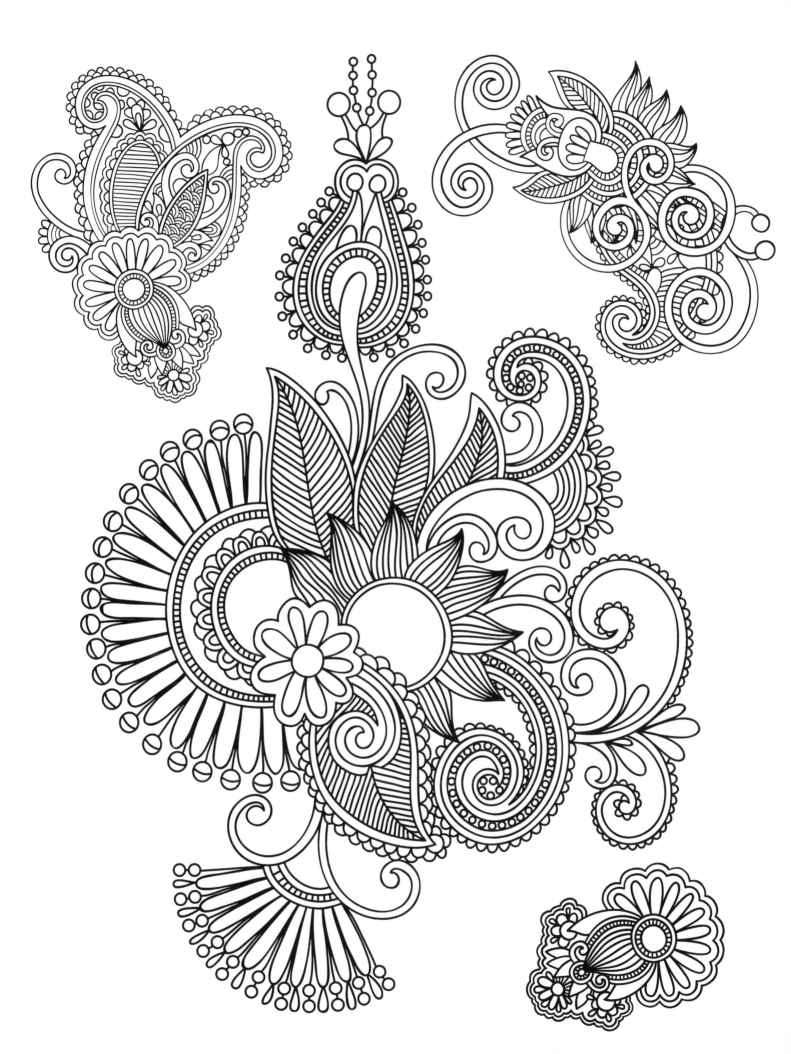

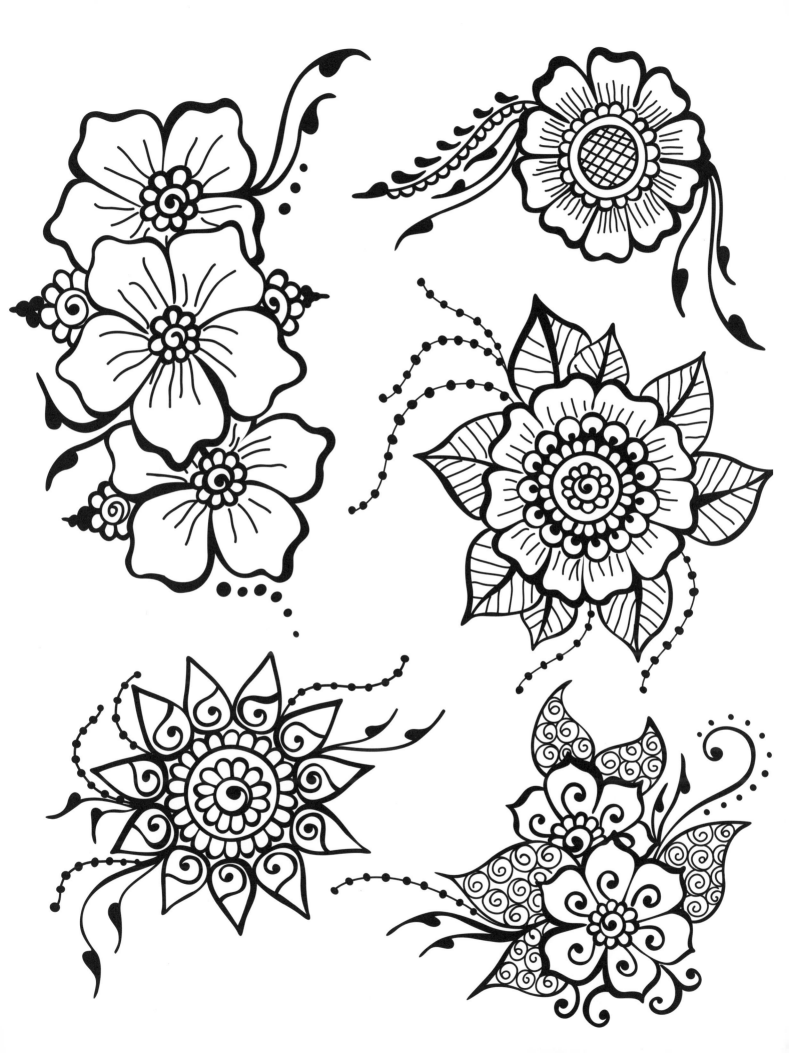

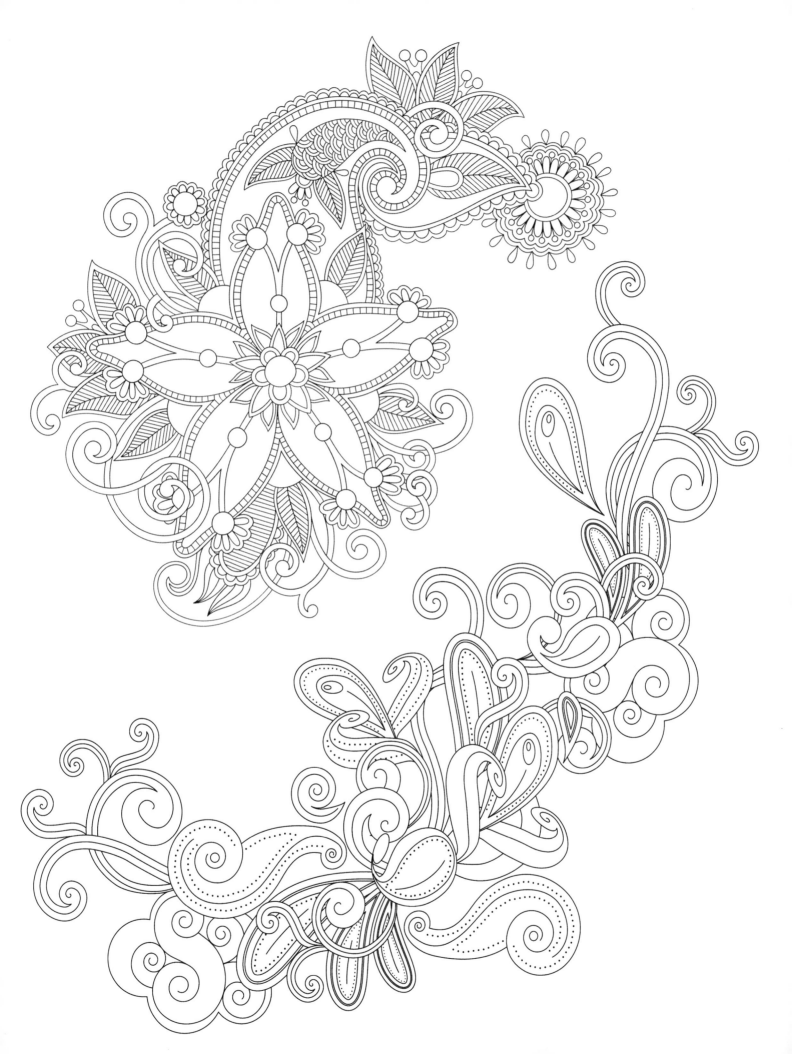

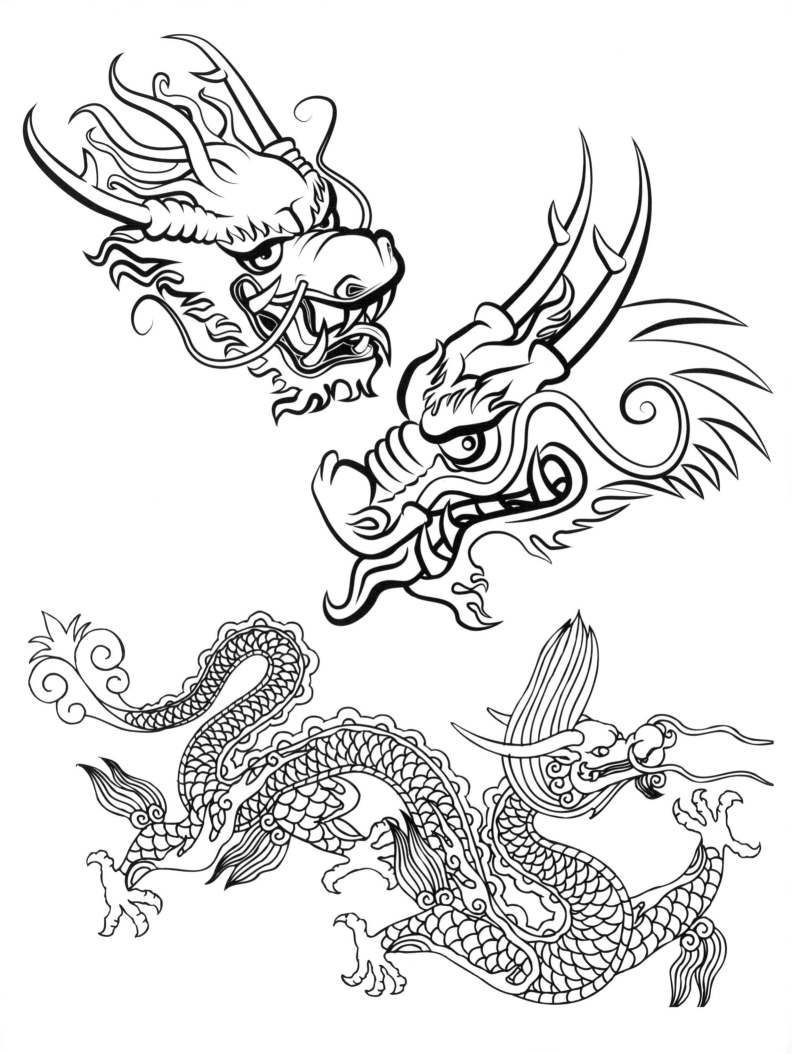

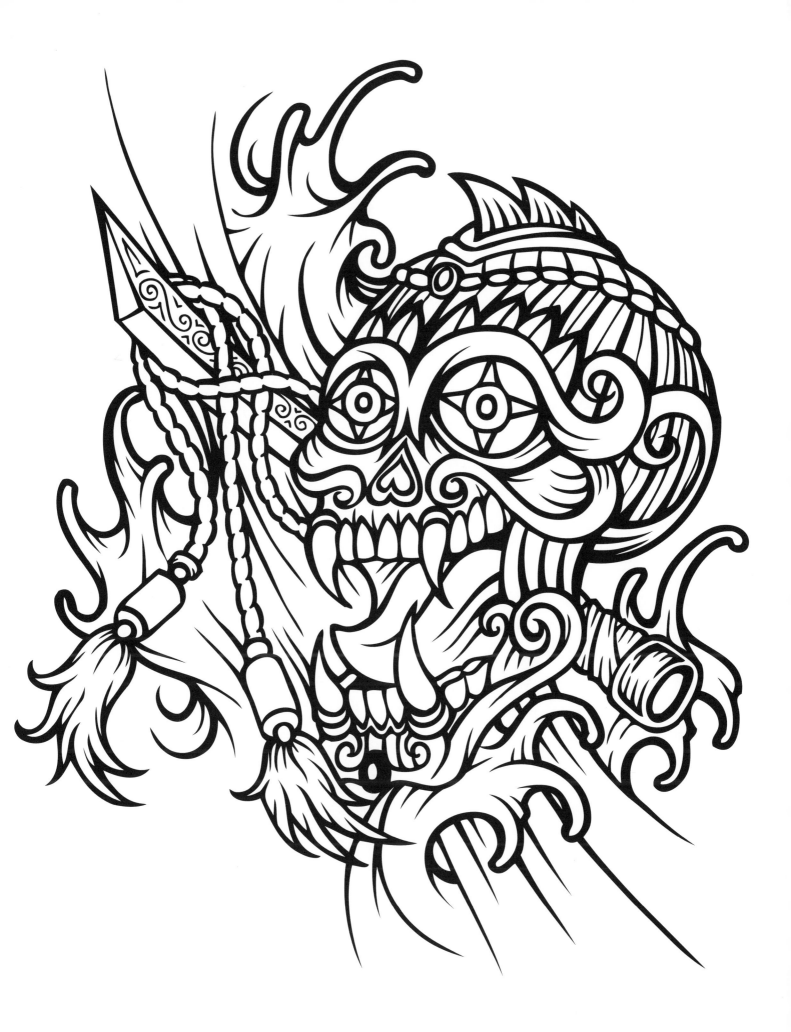

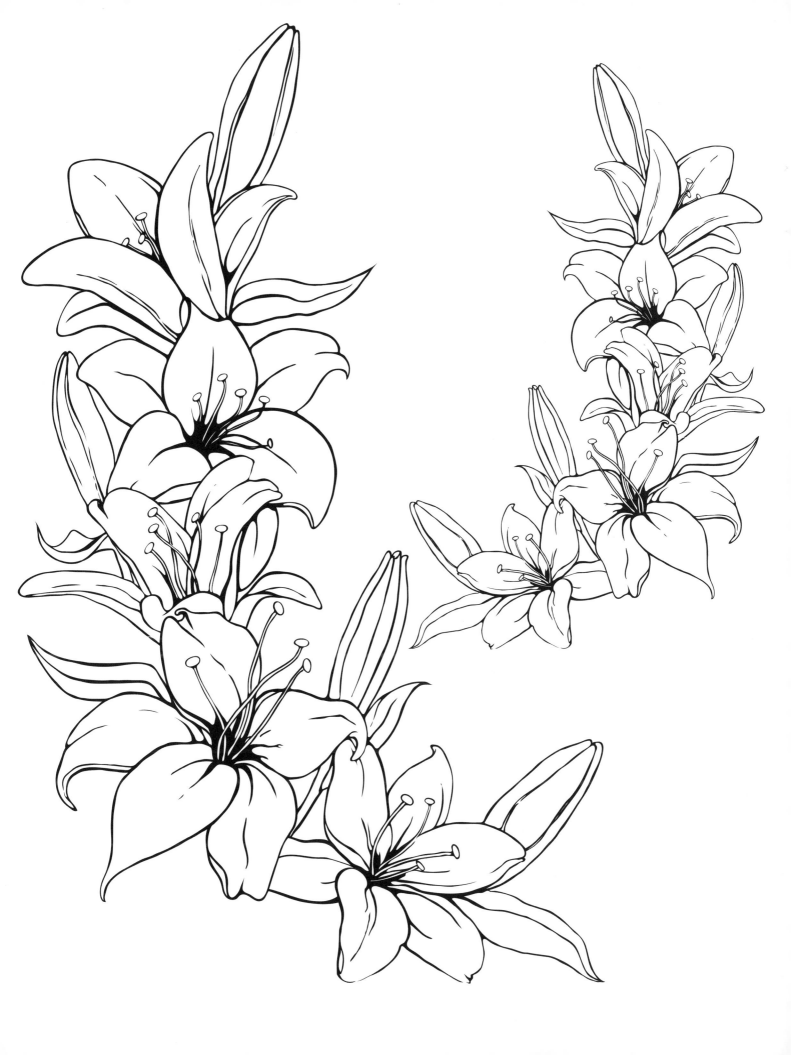

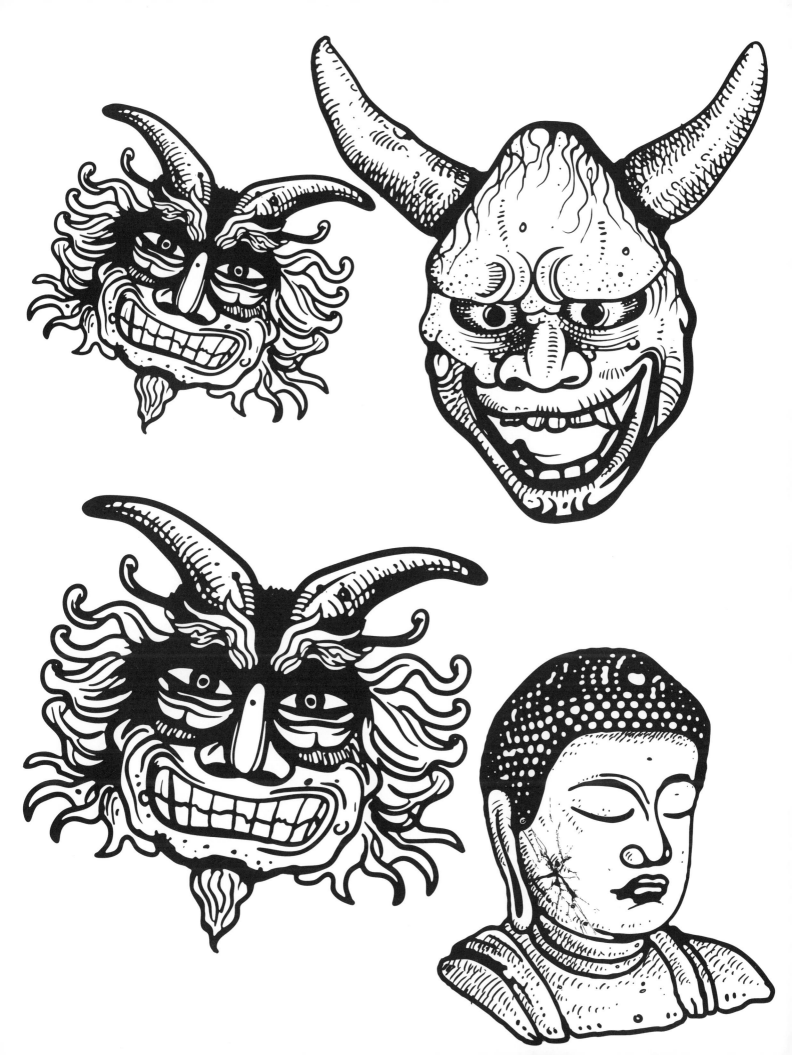

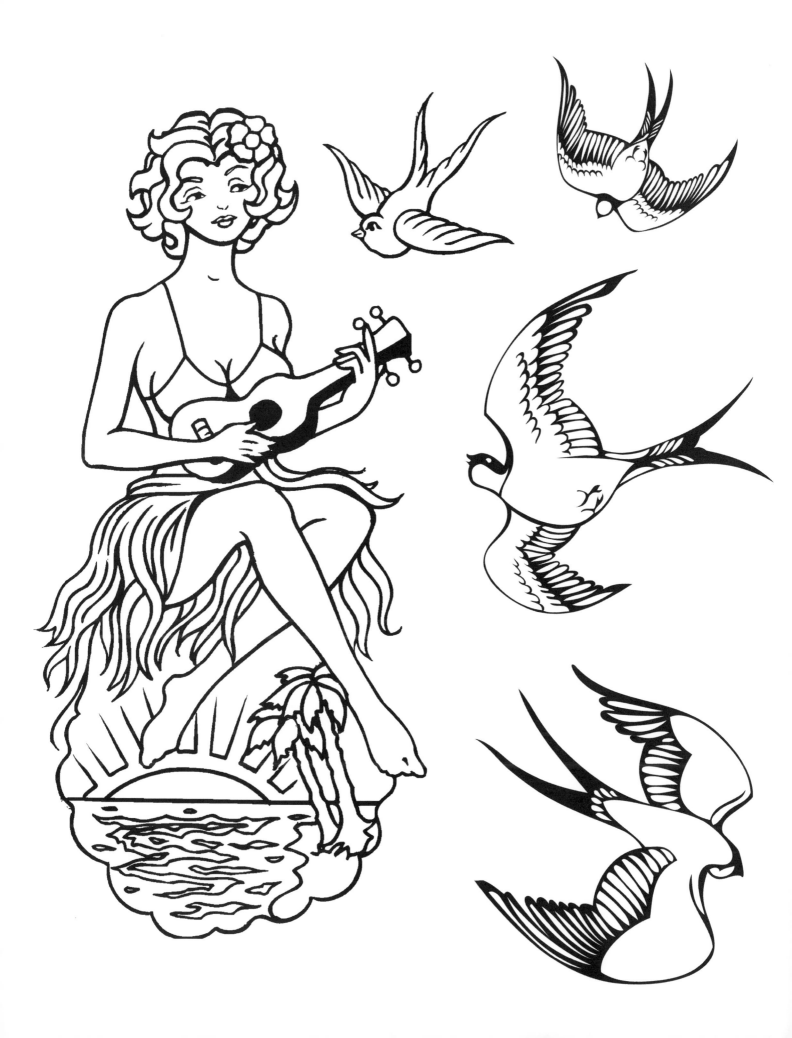

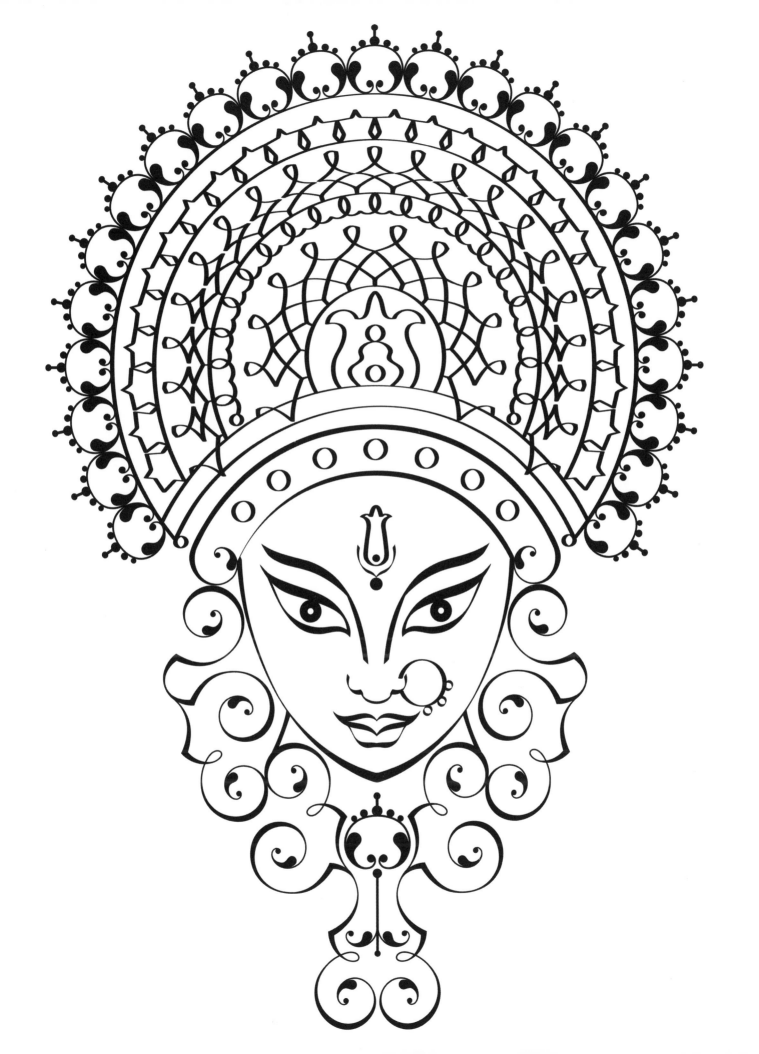

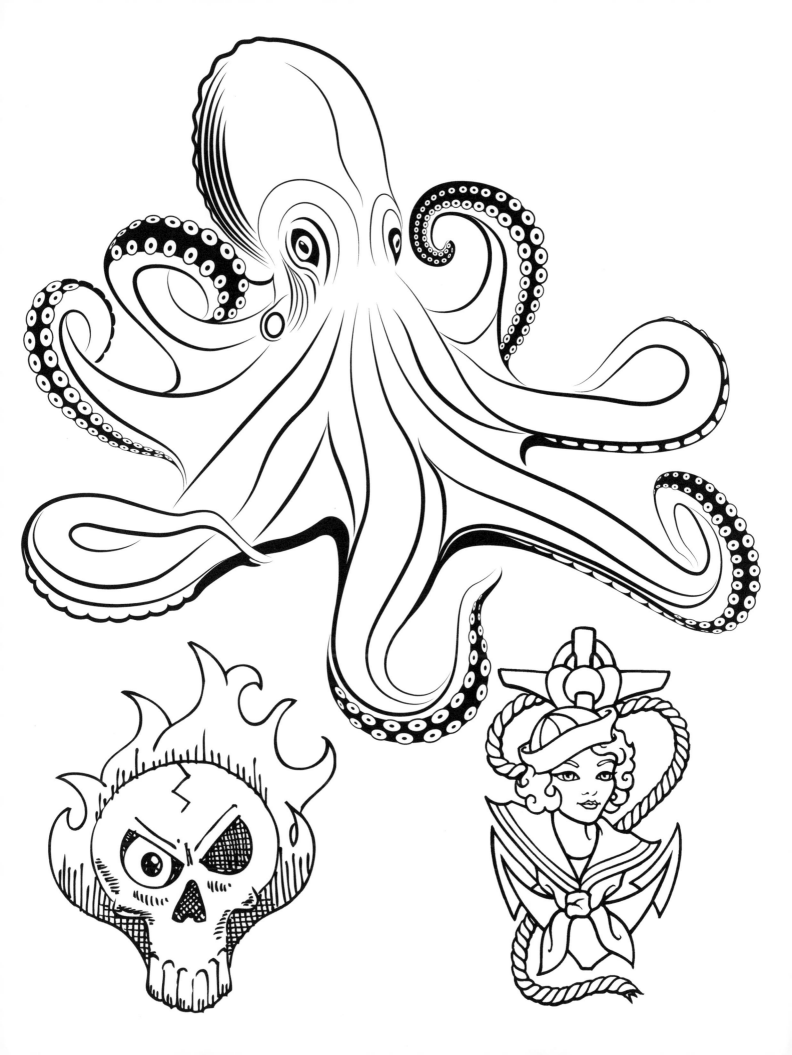

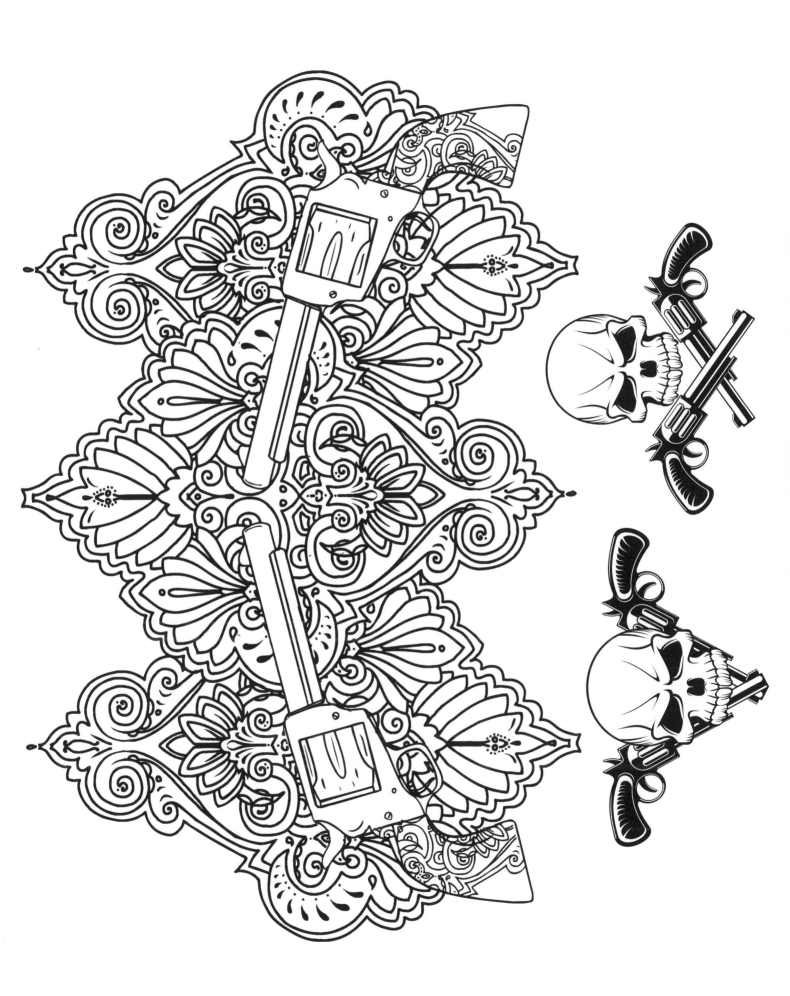

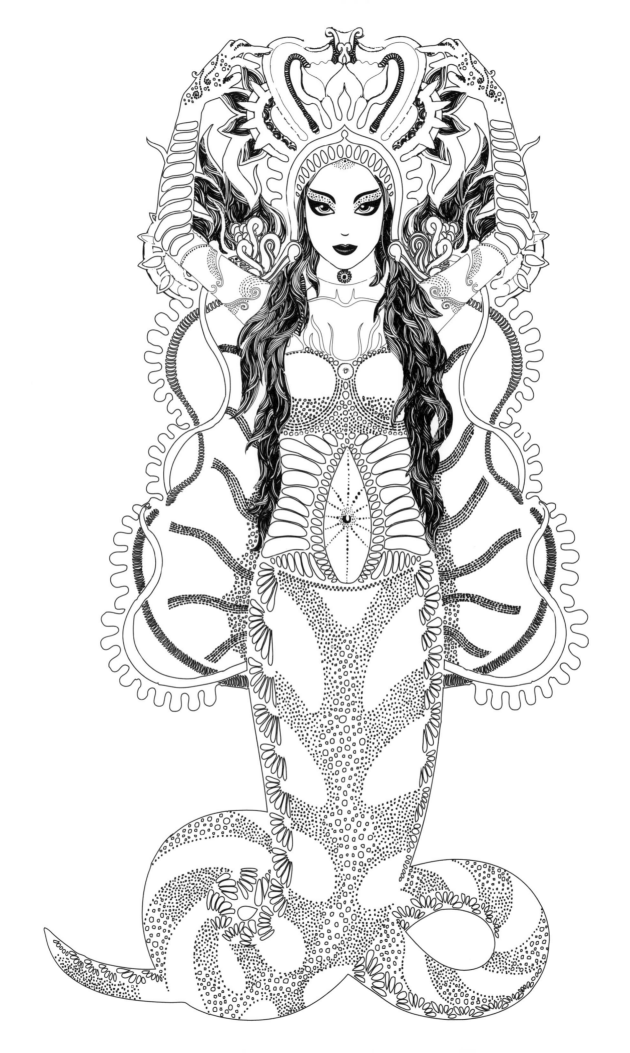

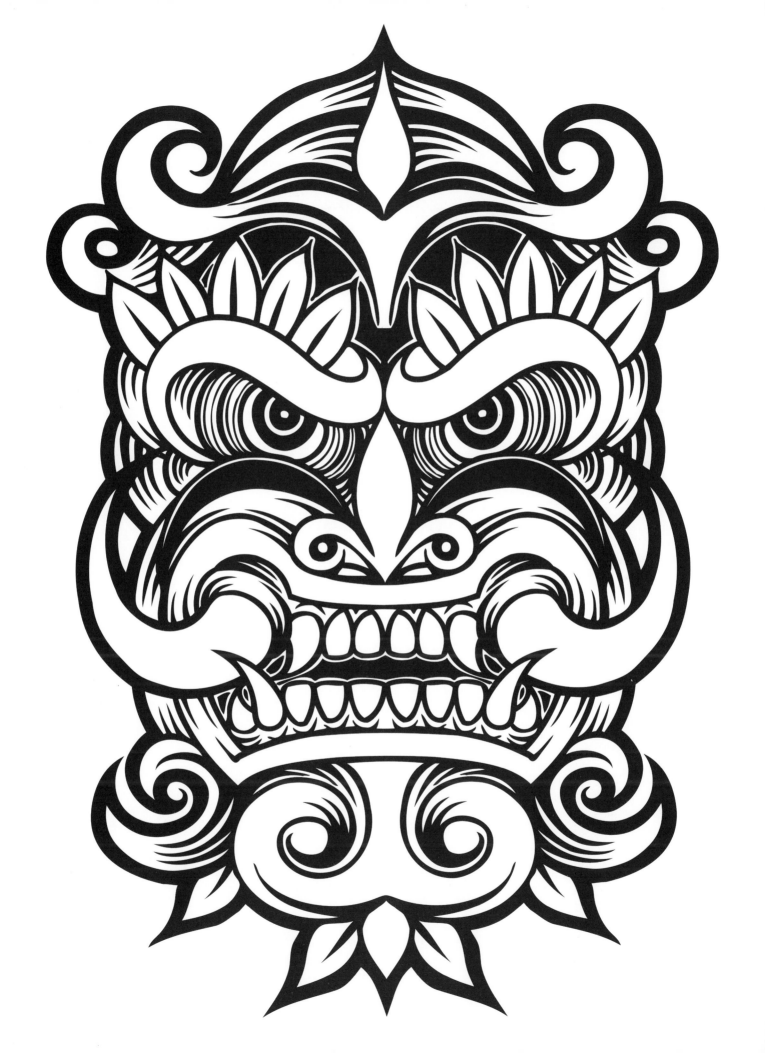

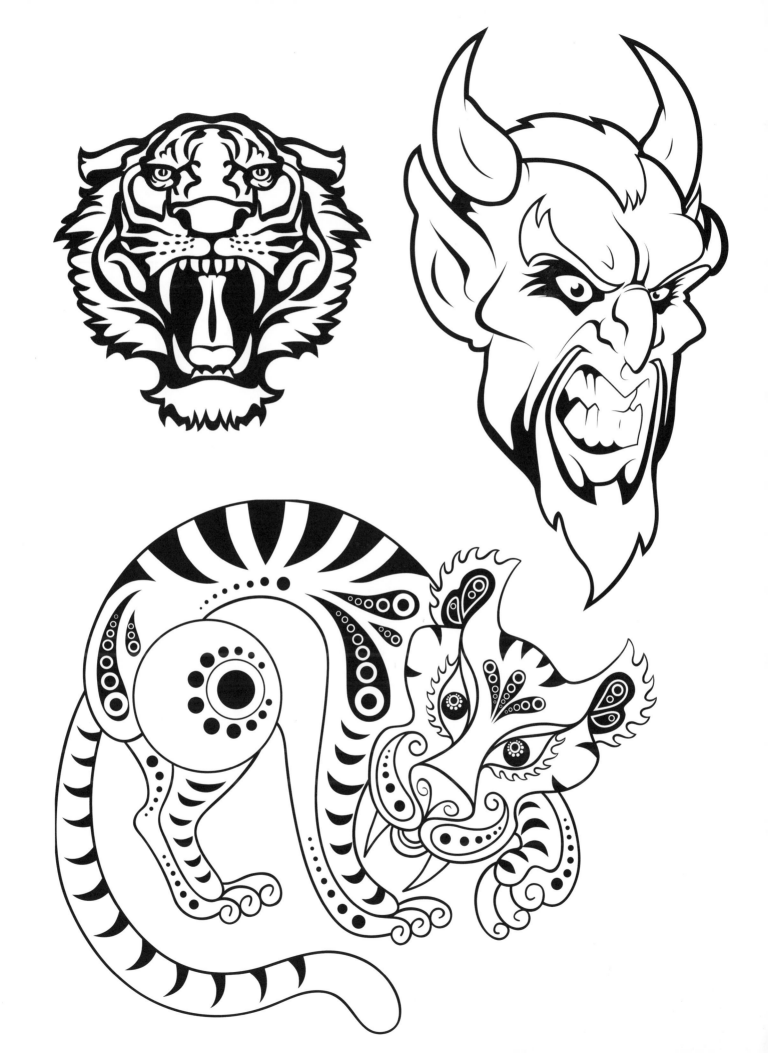

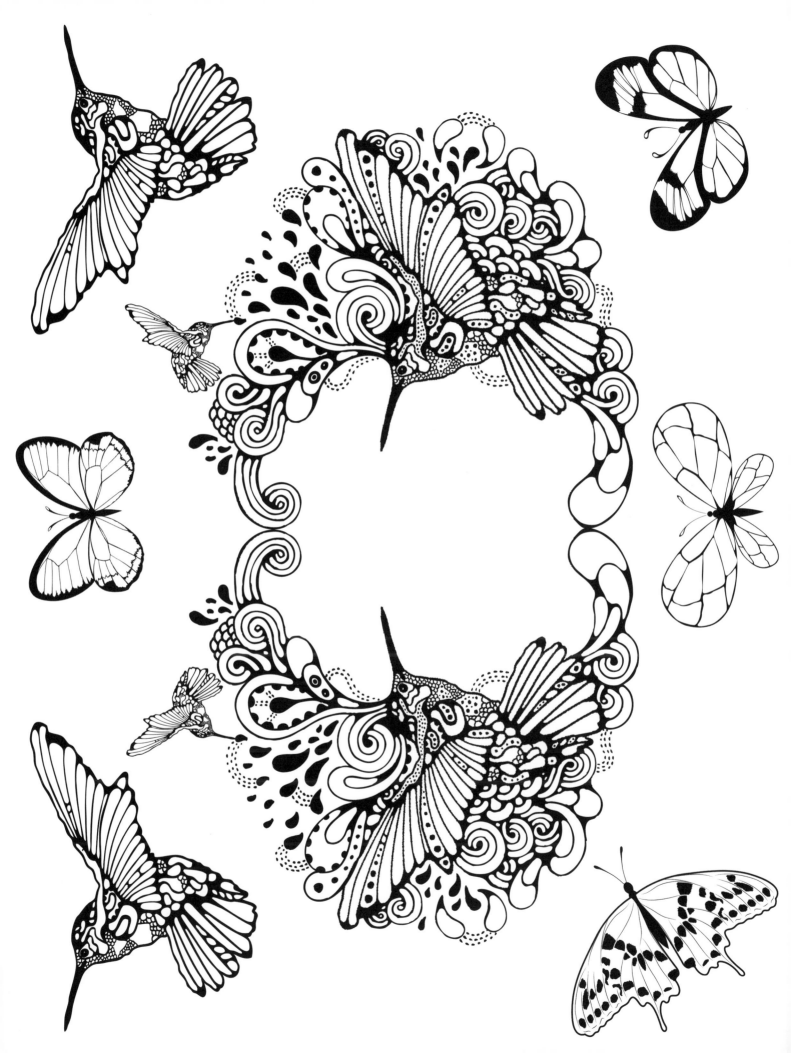

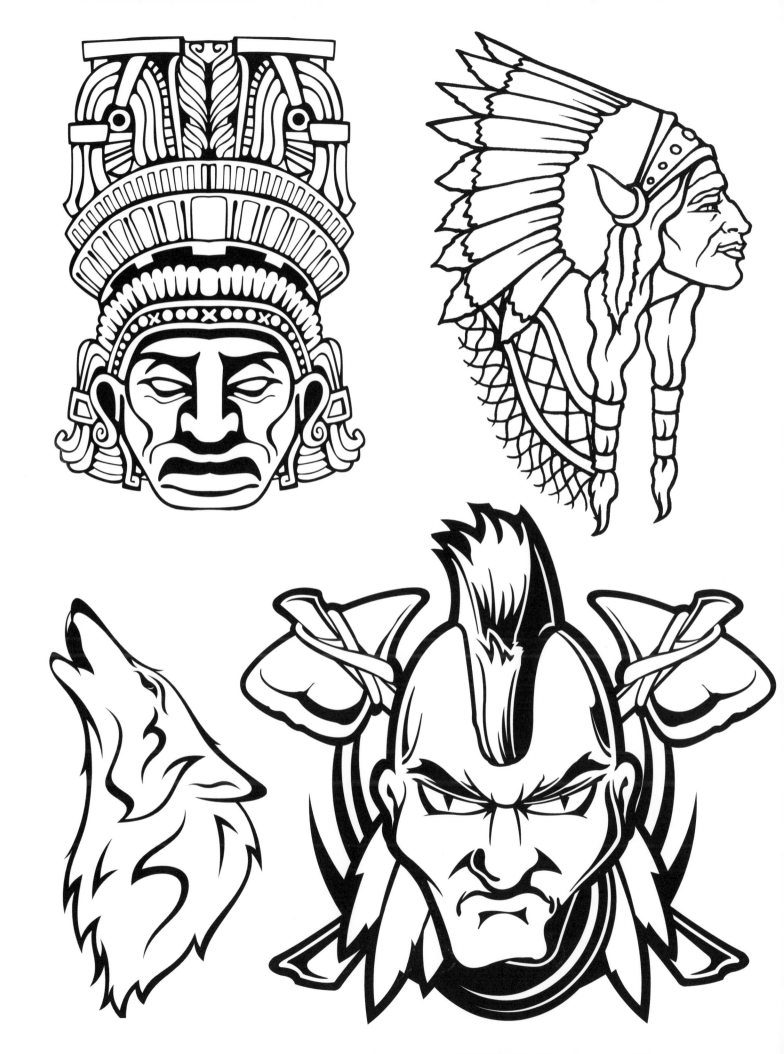

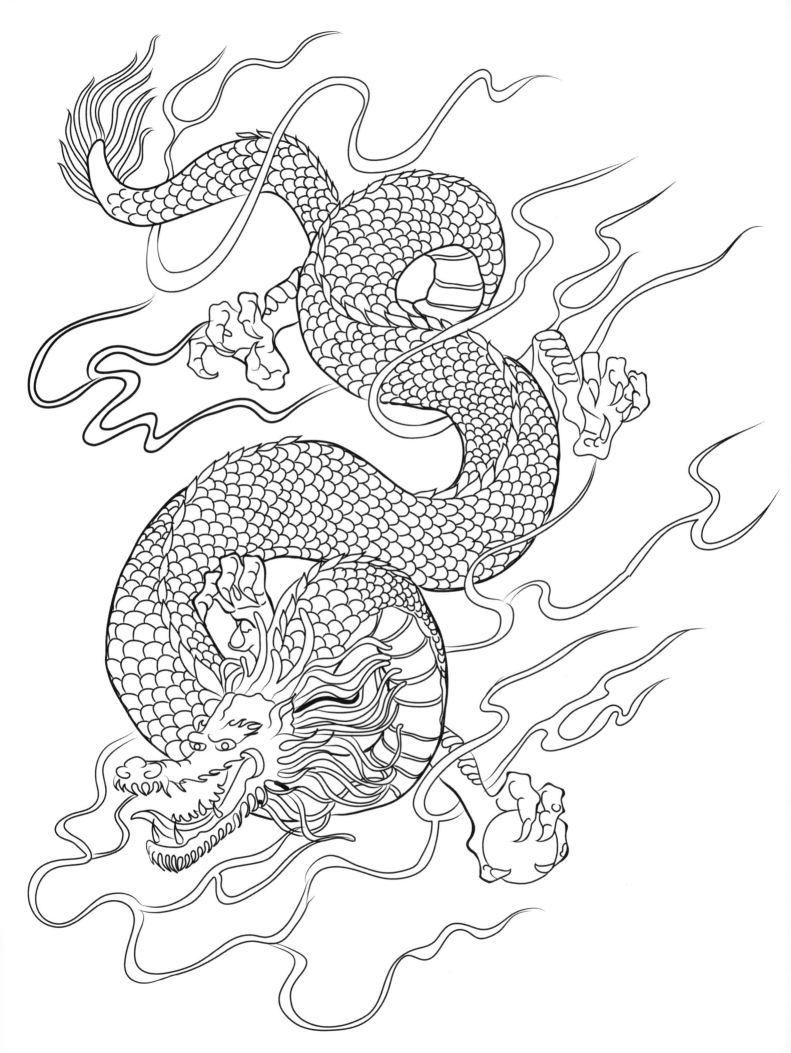

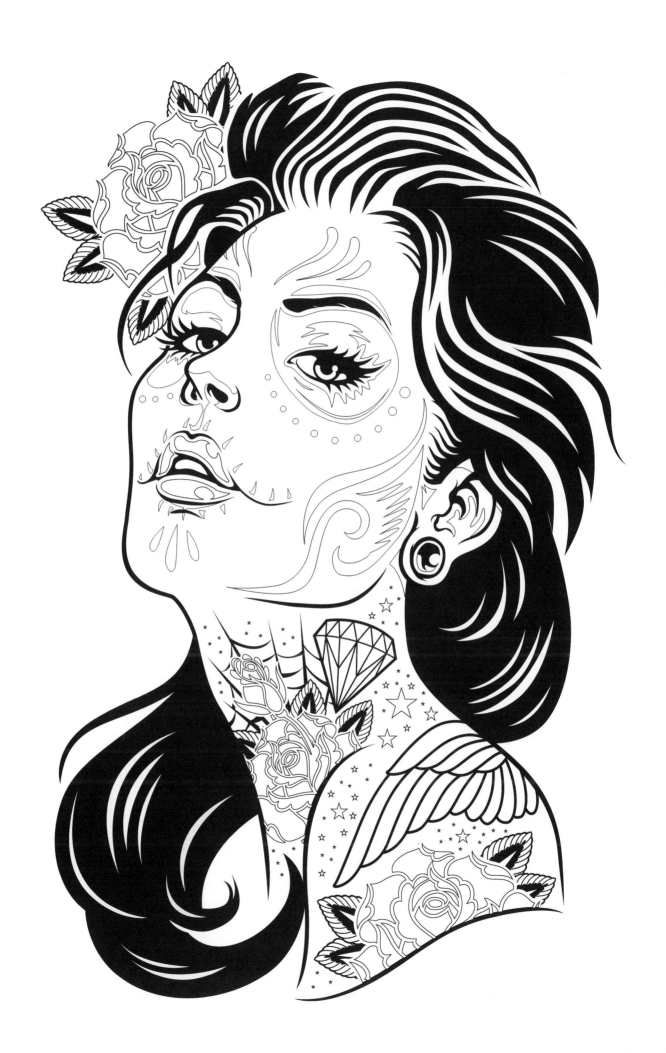

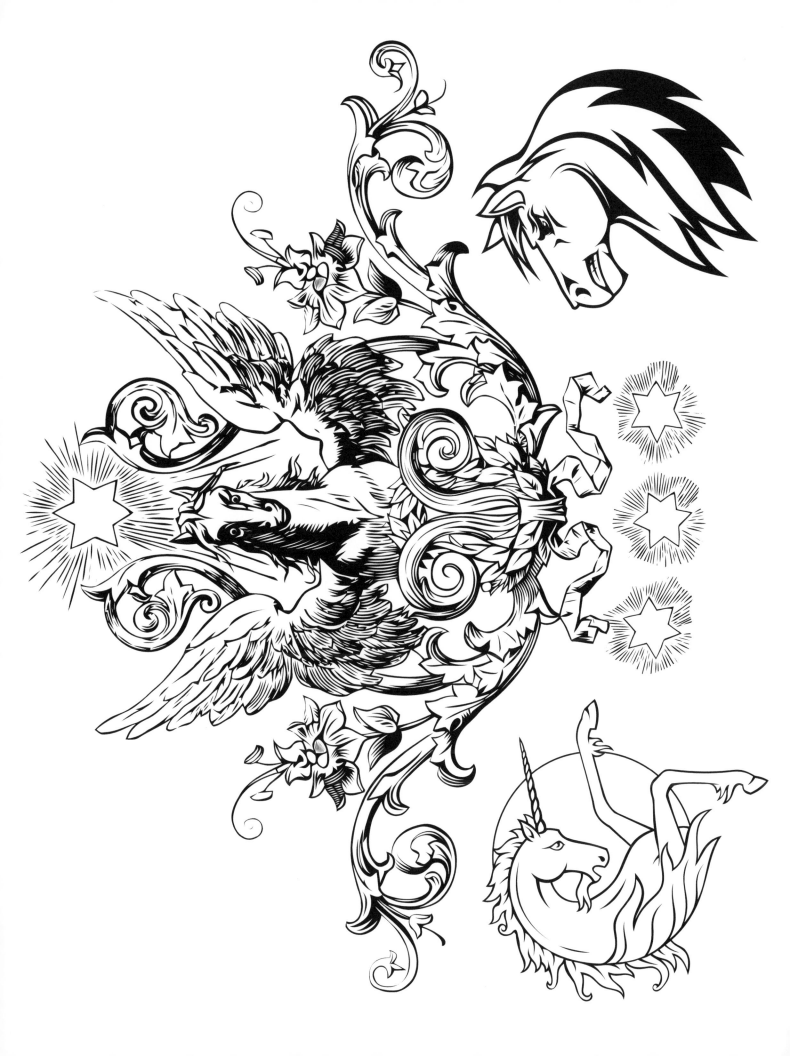

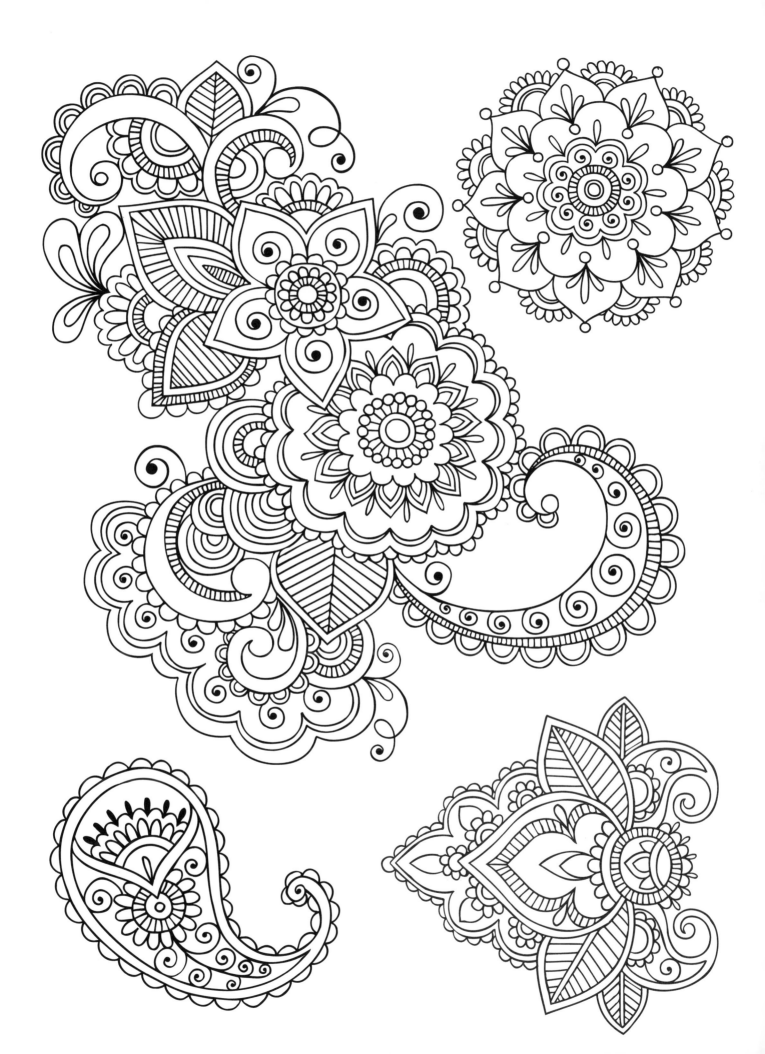

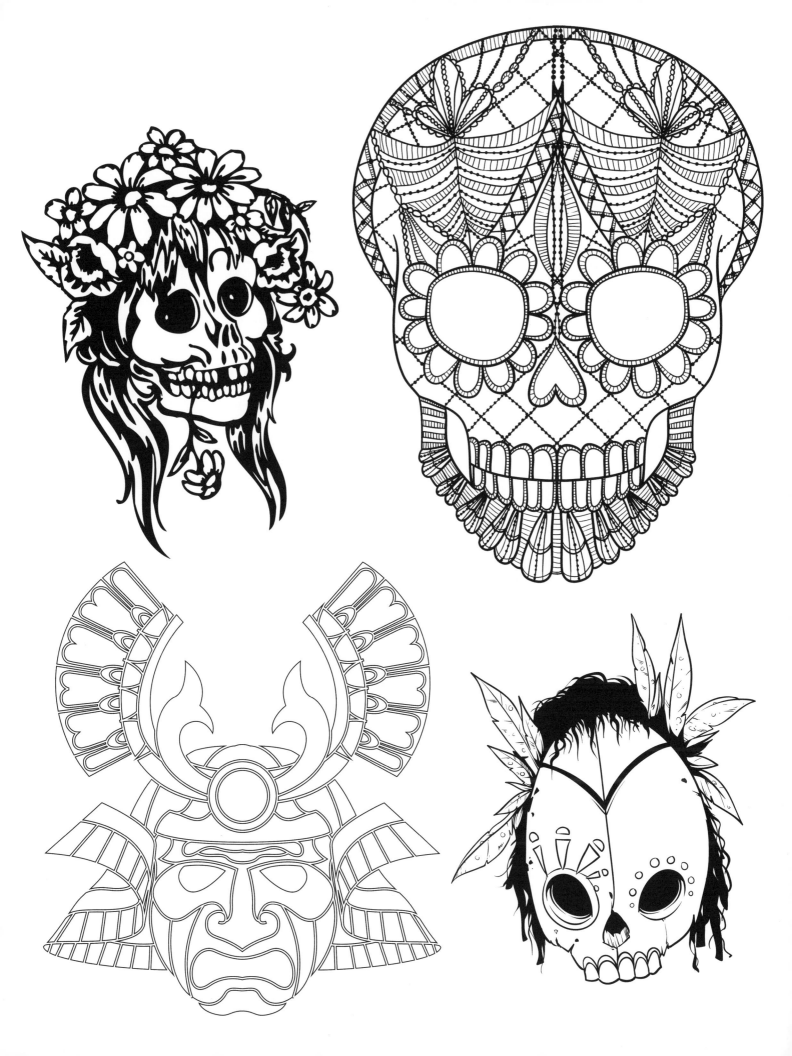